Handwriting is a systematic, observable hu.
childhood on, handwriting expresses conscious and unconscious *personal style* and principles of behavior well known to helping professionals and to our court system. Analytic graphology is a demonstrated psychological system.

Each person's writing style is unique because handwriting is expressive motion—a creative synthesis between brain, hand and eye which cannot be duplicated. Your handwriting IS you! And whether writing is "pretty" or not does not relate to a "pretty" character, but tells a lot about your potential creativity!

The *I* is the only letter which is symbolic of the self. Segments within its form also offer hints concerning innermost feelings about male and female roles and identities and how the writer may choose to identify with or relate to them.

Jane Green has, with her I study, brought one of the most valuable theories of the past decade to graphology in context of the totality of handwriting. She offers many well-illustrated case histories.
Rudolph S. Hearns, author of *Handwriting, an Analysis Through its Symbolism;* American correspondent for La Societe Francaise de Graphologie, Paris

HANDWRITING ANALYSIS THROUGH ANALYTIC GRAPHOLOGY CAN HELP YOU TO

make the most of your hidden assets
become more sensitive to others
recognize and conquer inner fears
encourage others

I recommend YOU & YOUR PRIVATE I as a superb teaching guide for both beginning and advanced graphology students.
Shirley Urbane, President, American Association of Handwriting Analysts

Jane Nugent Green

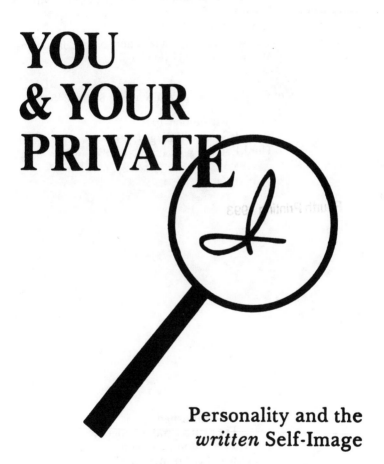

YOU
& YOUR
PRIVATE

Personality and the
written Self-Image

Third Edition, with Index
1988
Published by
Tyestring Productions
1760 Summit Avenue
Saint Paul, Minnesota 55105

Library of Congress Catalog Card Number: 83-080848

First Edition 1975
Second Edition, Enlarged, 1983
Third Edition, with Index, 1988

Fourth Printing 1993

Published by
Tyestring Productions
1760 Summit Avenue
Saint Paul, Minnesota 55105

Printed in the United States of America

CONTENTS

ACKNOWLEDGEMENT

This book has been a sharing experience. The development of my thinking about early parenting and male-female symbolism within the personal pronoun *I* has been aided by my study of competent graphologists who share my belief that graphology has a place in professional psychological personality assessment. I wish to thank them all, and especially wish to gratefully acknowledge the following: Leslie W. King, Ruth Bruce, Reverend Anthony J. Becker, Ph.D. (whose use of the term "sailboat *I*" began my investigations), Daniel Anthony, instructor at the New School for Social Research in New York City, British handwriting consultant Jane Paterson, author Rudolph Hearns, Felix Klein, Bertha Brown and Bette Gerber, my graphology partners Betty Link, Bette Lentsch, Jan Holthusen, and Questioned Documents Examiner Ann Hooten.

Writing sample of Joseph F. Nicollet was contributed by Martha Bray, editor of *The Journal of Joseph F. Nicollet: A Scientist on the Mississippi Headwaters with Notes on Indian Life.* (St. Paul, Minnesota: St. Paul Historical Society, 1970.)

Special thanks to Ann Wintrode, who compiled the Page Index to Fig. Illustrations.

A BRIEF HISTORY OF GRAPHOLOGY

Today in Europe, graphology is a required portion of the curriculum in many places. The University of Heidelberg, Kiel, and Munich, as well as schools in Holland, Switzerland, Italy and France all offer accredited work in the field.

Interest in handwriting as an indicator of character and personality appears to have existed since the eleventh century Chinese philosopher and painter Jo-Hau documented his observations. Two thousand years ago, comments concerning various Roman emperors' handwriting in relationship to their character were made. Cicero, Aristotle and Aesop were exponents of the art. The first systematic attempts to correlate handwriting with character were made in Italy at the beginning of the seventeenth century by Alderisius Prosper and court physician Camillo Baldo.

However, graphology as a systematic study has had a brief history. The term itself was unknown until 1871, when it was coined by Abbe Michon, who, with his teacher, Abbe Flandrin, began the French school of handwriting analysis. Michon used "fixed signs" in evaluating handwriting, and devoted a life-time to the study. Later, J. Crepieux-Jamin broke away from the limiting handwriting "signs" and approached the study from a more *Gestalt*, or over-all viewpoint. Further research was done by the famous French psychologist Alfred Binet (father of the intelligence test) and the psychiatrist Rogues de Fursac in the early twentieth century. Many other physicians and psychologists in France have carried on the study.

Toward the end of the nineteenth century, German scientists assumed leadership in graphology. Wilhelm Preyer, professor of physiology at Jena, suggested in 1895 that writing originates in the brain, not in the fingers: *hand*writing is actually *brain*writing. The neurologist Rudolf Pophal, professor emeritus of graphology at the University of Hamburg, furthered the systematic study, as did the brilliant Georg Meyer. Germany's most authoritative proponent was the philosopher Ludwig Klages, whose book, *Handwriting and Character* (1930) has been a leading force in the field. The basic theory Klages expressed was that handwriting movements actualize drives and tensions of the personality.

In Austria in the early thirties, the graphologists Rafael Schermann and Roda Wieser contributed further effort. The most outstanding proponent of the Swiss school was Dr. Max Pulver, a psychologist at the University of Zurich, who in 1934 discovered the three zones in handwriting. Finally, in England, Robert Saudek, Hans Jacoby and J. Eysenck produced further material regarding the validity of handwriting analysis.

Sigmund Freud, Carl Jung and Alfred Adler each recognized handwriting analysis because each was Gestalt-minded: they felt personality to be an over-all picture. (Alfred Adler referred to handwriting analysis often. Of *Handwriting Tells,* by Nadya Olyanova, he said, "Nadya Olyonova is to the science of graphology what Michelangelo is to painting.")

The wars in Europe created vast gaps in the continuity of graphological study. In the United States, handwriting analysis had a shaky existence. Although introduced by a number of European-trained physicians, neurologists and psychologists in the thirties, much American graphology found its way immediately to the field of entertainment. In spite of this, some research was eventually accomplished by such men as the psychologist Gordon Allport and his co-worker Philip Vernon. The late Dr. Erich Alten of New York was a pioneer in the use of handwriting analysis in the practice of medicine. In the forties, extensive work was done by Thea Stein Lewinson and Joseph Zubin in measurements relating to handwriting components and contraction-release.

Psychology professor Werner Wolff and Ulrich Sonneman, a clinical psychologist, added notable contributions on form level and rhythm. The late Klara Roman, who taught graphology at the New School for Social Research in New York City was an acknowledged leader from abroad. Microscope and slow-action film, measurement of pen-pressure and other devices have been used in the scientific study of handwriting. Daniel

Anthony, a student of Klara Roman, has continued to teach courses at the New School on college level, as well as becoming a recognized expert in the field of personnel selection through graphology.

Dr. Herry O. Teltscher, a European-trained psychologist and psychotherapist, has written extensively on validation studies of graphology. Alfred Kanfer has spent over thirty years investigating possible links between cancer and handwriting at the Strang Clinic in New York. Rudolph Hearns has done research on handwriting and dyslexia. Many other American graphologists are presently engaged in furthering the cause of graphology; most of the experts, however, are from abroad.

Lags in handwriting analysis exist in part because of the different approaches used by European and American psychologists. European psychological research has dealt primarily with the subjective; American research—under the influence of stimulus-response Behaviorism—has dealt primarily with the objective. Projective techniques have not commonly been in use in America, nor favorably received for the most part. (At the International Congress of Handwriting Psychology held in Amsterdam in 1966, only two American delegates were native-born out of the three hundred from eighteen countries represented. The greatest attendance was from Germany, France and the Netherlands.)

American studies are handicapped by the fact that there is not yet a licensing clearing house or caretaker agency to ensure due competence of practising graphologists. Furthermore, graphology is not yet an established part of the graduate psychology curriculum, and there is currently little expert aid in translating the expanding body of experimental research being done abroad. Financial gains from the practice of graphology are not marked, although computerized graphology for entertainment has rapidly caught on as a money-maker.

However, graphology as a new tool for personnel selection is moving into the field. Emotional make-up, motivation, self-confidence, sense of responsibility and other factors of character can be determined through handwriting analysis and used to supplement other psychological testing devices. Today an increasing number of firms in the United States are using graphology in this manner. Much of this is not publicized, but it exists and is continuing to prove its usefulness.

One important change has been the removal of analytic graphology from *occult* listing in the library Dewey Decimal System. The index entry now places most of it at 155.282 (Individual psychology). Classifications are 155.282 (Diagnostic graphology), 363.2565 (Documentary evidence) and 658.3112 (Selection of Personnel by management).

Rose Matousek, a Professional Life Member of the American Association of Handwriting Analysts, was instrumental in accomplishing this task through the Library of Congress in 1980. This is a giant step forward in closing the credibility gap and encouraging valid graphological research and study.

It is heartening to report that variations in American copybook have *not* invalidated the graphological principles or hypothesis concerning male-female symbols expressed in the first edition of *You and Your Private I*. On the contrary, reliable evidence continues to mount through consensual validation by reputable graphologists. No reliable theory of opposite symbolic placement appears to be credible.

Writing actions are intrinsic to history. Symbolic expressions of the self represented by the personal pronoun *I* involve social and cultural influences as well as changing sexual roles and role-models. Just as change is inherent in personality development, changing school copybooks authentically reflect new ways of being and acting.

In some capital *I* copybook forms, the importance and scope of the female role is emphasized by upper loop dominance, often without, or with lessened, male finishing strokes. However, most copybook *I's* still start with a leftward movement to the right. Few school systems accept a copybook *I* written like a small letter *l*. Even within that simplified form, directional qualities portray both male and female influences to the trained eye. (See *Symbolism and the Why of the I*).

Most copybook *I* forms continue to be written with both hard and soft strokes. Copybook changes indicated by forming larger middle zone areas of small letters may be relevant to the growing fact that more women are entering the American work forces. In spite of many changes, the art, science and symbolism of analytic graphology is continually appropriate to the study of human personality.

So far as the self-image goes, the written personal pronoun I continues to stand as a unique symbol of the self which is quite different from the capital copybook I. The term, *ppI*, appears to be a valid differentiating description.

PART I

THE WRITTEN
SELF-IMAGE

Chapter 1

MORE THAN THE MESSAGE

One day an instructor in a college communications class gave each of his students a copy of a composition written by a sixth grader who had been asked to describe what she saw in a certain picture. In the picture, a small cat, fur on end, was streaking for a nearby tree with a large black dog in hot, but obviously vain, pursuit. The college students were asked to "react" to the single written page given to them.

The responses were varied. One student merely said, "It's the usual description of a dog chasing a cat." Another stated, "I think the writer of this composition is very imaginative because she made up a complete story—gave the animals names and established a long-time feud between them."

Perhaps the most perceptive comment came from a young man named Bob, who said, "There's more than the dog-chasing-cat message in this one. I feel as though I know quite a lot about the girl who wrote this, just by looking at the paper. See how splotchy it is—it looks a lot like my own handwriting. A high school math teacher once asked me if I did my algebra with a charcoal briquet." The class laughed. "This sixth grader's handwriting seems unusually large—it runs off the page on the righthand side even though there's plenty of room at the bottom of the page. I'd say off-hand that this girl wasn't a very good planner."

Unknowingly, Bob had touched upon two aspects of handwriting: the conscious and the unconscious, both of which use symbols, each in a very special way. The dictionary defines a symbol as something that stands for, or represents, something else.

Words are among our most common symbols. Generally, we know what they represent, and we use them with awareness of what we are doing. We are also involved with conscious symbols when we salute the flag, wear a wedding ring, shake hands, or hang a horseshoe over a doorway. It is common knowledge what these actions symbolize.

The unconscious use of symbols is not so easy to illustrate, because unconscious symbols come in various disguises. For instance, it is not unusual for a person to describe a dream and then wonder what it means. However, a great deal of the time we do not know we are using unconscious symbols, or even that they are symbols. Bob's evaluation of the sixth-grader's composition dealt with unconscious symbolism which the writer did not intend to communicate. As Bob said, the page of writing was "more than the message."

The art of graphology, or handwriting analysis, is concerned with symbolic communication. Symbolism in handwriting expresses an added dimension, a plus-factor which conveys a subjective, personal quality beyond the basic existence of the writing. Handwriting is not simply manufactured, like identical cars on an assembly line. Writing design is not random, but unconsciously significant to the writer. It appears that to a certain extent we obey the "rules" of our inner system of symbols. Personal symbols are rarely neutral: they are caused by or evoke feelings which are part of the personality. Private pictures lie within the structure of writing forms.

It has been said that expressive movement is lockstitched into the fabric of personality. A forger finds his individuality a handicap and may practice writing upside-down and backwards in the hope of eliminating the telltale tracks of his own handwriting.

"We live by symbols," said Justice Oliver Wendell Holmes. The symbol with which this book is concerned is the written symbol of the ego, the personal pronoun *I* , the most important letter in the alphabet to each of us. The ego can be defined as the conscious self—the feeling, knowing and willing *I*, unique and separate from all other persons in the world.

One psychoanalyst described the ego as an island on the sea of the conscious, which in turn is an island on the larger sea of the unconscious. For the purposes of this book, the ego is truly an *I*-land.

And it is to this fascinating, often mysterious, Everyman's *I*-land that the following chapters will take you on a first-time graphological exploration.

Chapter 2

THE SIGNIFICANCE OF FORM

At twenty-one, Fred D. was a young man with a winning smile and a dashing kind of boldness. He was broad-shouldered, handsome and alert. The graphologist could understand his fiancee's pride as she showed off his photograph or talked about him.

Theirs had been a sudden, fast-paced romance that surprised Anne's parents, who were accustomed to tradition and formality. Undaunted, she set the wedding date, just two months after meeting Fred.

"Look," she said one day, her face aglow, "Look what he wrote to me--and sent special delivery."

It was a very short note. Just a few lines, in fact. But part of it seemed particularly significant. Look at Figure 1 on the following page. Fred's personal pronoun *I* contrasts strikingly with his large and flamboyant signature. The tiny slanted stroke is skeletonized, dwarfed by the larger letters around it. As the graphologist gazed at its stark bareness, it was easy to see that Fred's ego symbol--his personal pronoun *I*--was a symbol of despair. In spite of his outward confidence, it appeared that Fred had failed to establish a satisfactory inner sense of self-worth.

Although Fred did reach out toward other people (as his handwriting motion indicates), it was only in retaliation for his deeper feelings of inadequacy. For there were other handwriting clues to indicate tension, fear and hostility.

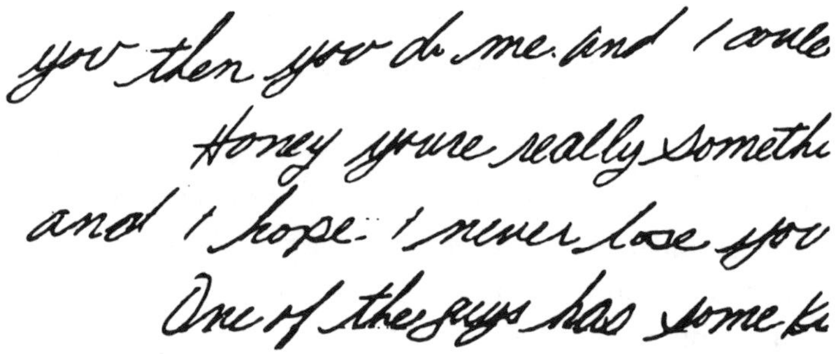

Fig. 1

For Anne's sake, the graphologist hoped this unexpressed analysis was completely wrong. Unfortunately, it was sadly accurate. Fred walked out—just the day before the wedding. He left another note, this one saying he wasn't good enough for her, that he couldn't go through with it. That was all. Anne was heartbroken. She couldn't understand it.

If she had known the facts about Fred's earlier life (which she learned much later), Anne might have understood a little better. The private Fred was quite different from his public image. Fred felt he had been a hated child. Countless times his alcoholic father had told him he was no good. His mother, who worked to bring money into the household, said she loved her son, but seldom demonstrated affection for him for fear of "making him a homosexual." After a school record of failure and truancy, he ran away from home at the age of thirteen.

The eloquent vocabulary of handwriting—*form, size, movement, pressure*—reveals aspects of Fred's inner self in the single stroke of his personal pronoun *I*. Popular opinion in America is suspicious of any quick and easy diagnosis of personality—and rightly so. The time will never come when a handwriting analyst can glance at a writing and tell Mrs. Jones whether her son will become a happy, successful man or a sad failure.

But the time has come when the study of a single letter, the personal pronoun *I*, can provide a trained graphologist additional insight into a writer's character and personality. As in Fred's case, a study of the pp*I* (personal pronoun *I*) can indeed show trouble brewing or already present.

Words, we know, are symbols by which we communicate what we see, hear, smell, touch, think or feel. Form, too, is a language. The gnarled and stunted manzanita tree of California tells us a story quite different from the stately Norway pine of northern Minnesota. The shape of a greyhound suggests speed; the squatness of the English bulldog, power and tenacity. Our body has a language apart from words or form. How one walks, sits, gestures, is *body language* which speaks a clear message of gaiety, sadness or anxiety—the inner state of being.

Like body language, writing strokes are forms in action. They express inner reactions on the part of the writer. You cannot divorce yourself from personal involvement when you create or observe certain designs or patterns.

Do you like the restfulness of this stroke?
Are you more attracted to this stroke?
Is it easy for you to make this design?
What do you think about this pattern?

You will see them again throughout this book. Such strokes are found in both art and handwriting. Human action involves form-making.

The structure of form is so significant to mankind that some designs have remained meaningful throughout human history. The "magic circle" mandala, for example, is a symbol of wholeness dating from prehistoric times. This symbol, drawn by cavemen, is being worn today in modified form around the necks of the younger generation as a symbol of peace and unity. Psychologists have discovered that the unchanged form of a circled cross is still being drawn spontaneously all over the world by children of all cultures as they achieve maturity in putting design on paper.

A child completing a mud-pie experiences a pleasure known also to the sophisticated sculptor. Each gains satisfaction from trying to make something. In creating forms—be they mud-pies or statues, buildings or gardens—a part of the person involved is released and expressed. Form-making is self-extension, self-projection. It requires decisions by the maker. These are profoundly personal decisions, acts of creation which may have universal significance, and always have private meaning as well.

The term "form" has added meaning for the graphologist. Handwriting may be classified from *low* form level to *high* form level. Determining this level of form requires training, experience and judgment. It means careful study of the over-all writing pattern. For instance, the simplified personal pronoun *I* (pp*I*) can be found in handwritings of both very high and very low form level.

Form is related in some measure to what we think of ourselves. Each writing form is expressive movement of a personal nature. Recognizable aspects of this expression are movements which are distinctive enough to differentiate one individual from another. No matter how stereotyped it appears, each letter has been brought into being through a unique continuum of the writer's brain and body, even if the writing instrument by necessity is held with the toes or the mouth.

Naturalness, originality, and aesthetic balance in the use of space contribute to the pleasing aspects of writing of a high form level. Other graphic elements such as rhythm, overall simplification, balance of letters, firmness of the writing stroke (ductus) indicate the quality of the form level. Lack of these positive qualities in the script are indications of a low form level, suggesting an inharmonious personality on the part of the writer.

The *I* symbol cannot be divorced from its surrounding form level any more than one isolated personality trait can identify a subject. For example, simplified *I*'s which depart from copybook models are found in the script of persons of completely different character. The graphic value of a particular simplified form lies within the total framework of the handwriting; simplicity alone can have no specific identifying value.

Consider the following two examples of writing form. In the one, the simple, open *I* is a sign of genuine originality—in the other, a sign of traumatic protest.

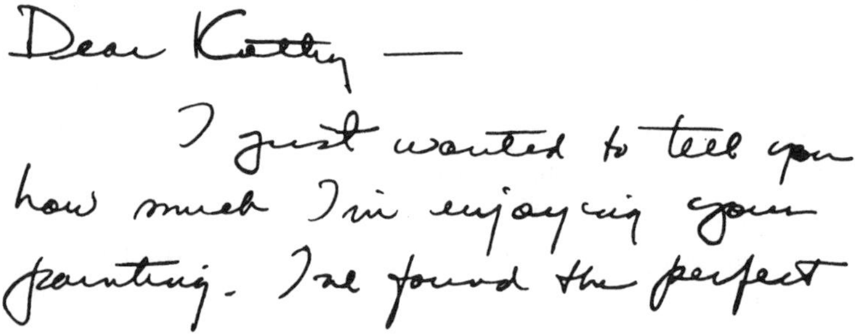

Fig. 2

Figure 2 is written by a creative artist and author. The simplified personal pronoun *I* is in harmony with the rest of the original and simplified letter formations within the text.

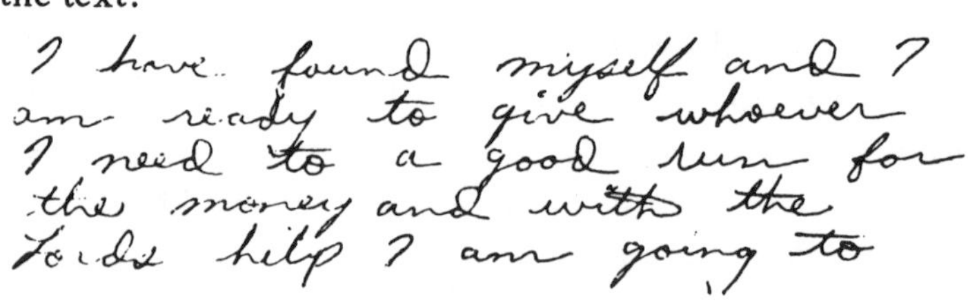

Fig. 3

Figure 3 is the writing of a young man indicted for

the stabbing murder of a young girl. Sparseness of the *I* reinforces the over-all disharmony within the text, indicated by the jumpy, split pressure, overblown loops, erratic spacing, and tremulous ductus. The whole writing clearly suggests conflicts and personality difficulties.

Although the ego symbol—the personal pronoun *I*—appears equally simple in each writing sample, the implications of each graphic form are totally different.

How the pp*I* (personal pronoun *I*) is written and where it is placed on the paper reveal the writer's intimate attitudes about himself and others. How he signs his name, on the other hand, is less revealing. The public image, represented by the signature does not reveal—and may even at times deny—the truth about a person suggested by his personal pronoun.

How you form your pp*I* can offer you a useful tool for assessing your private needs and values. In revealing aspects of the inner self, it has a personal meaning beyond the ordinary fact that it denotes the writer. It can also suggest harmonious or disturbing elements within a person's life. It can reveal the importance of the male and female authority figures to the writer and how his relationship with these figures affect his present dealings.

Mind and body are not independent units or entities: expressive movements are embedded in the total complex of the personality. Writing becomes disorganized when the will is not in control—writing appearance will change if you are drunk, drugged or drowsy. Handwriting is so personal a gesture that imitating or forging is difficult to do, and writing speed and pressure cannot be duplicated. *Hand*-writing is *brain*-writing.

As one ages physically, the written forms have a tendency to become more rigid and stressful; nevertheless, actual age cannot be told from handwriting form. Nor is sex or left- or right-handedness reliably revealed. Many women are considered "masculine" in our society. Many men, particularly the creative ones, have writing which appears to have feminine qualities. Certainly, one's fortune or future cannot be told from one's handwriting. For instance, a successful salesman may be driven to compete in the same sense as the "unsuccessful" man. Handwriting cannot reveal what each person will do with his traits.

Personality involves a conglomerate of behavior traits interrelated into a recognizable whole. The values which a person maintains cannot be precisely measured, for their effect upon life can be assessed only in comparison with other values affecting the total personality structure. The image you carry of yourself is likewise built up of many factors blending into a unified picture.

In similar fashion, graphological skill is based upon the analyst's perception of patterns as they *relate to each other*. The graphic patterns you write reflect your self-awareness on both a conscious and an unconscious level. This aggregate of design cannot be successfully evaluated in separate pieces—accurate judgment must be based upon the entire structure rather than on isolated traits. A stroke of the pen has more than one interpretation: Positive, negative or just a ho-hum effect depending on the over-all graphological picture. Tendencies are not fixed traits; the human personality has an unknown number of variables fluctuating within the synergized whole. Handwriting cannot simply pigeonhole or label an individual. For example, there is no such thing as a classic "criminal" handwriting or "homosexual" handwriting per se.

The sense of self is a constantly unfolding, evolving thing throughout the human life. The psychiatrist Carl Jung called it "the miracle of the I." Each person is the *uncarven image* in the block of marble. And what each will eventually carve will depend largely upon his private self-image, that significant cornerstone of personality.

And what is your private self-image? It is your concept about yourself.

Consciously, you know what you look like, you know the things you enjoy, you know how you wish to appear to others. This aspect of yourself is not too difficult to discern.

Unconsciously, too, you have knowledge about who you are and what you are. But this private, unconscious self-knowledge—your self-concept—is not readily known, either to yourself or to others. As in the case of Fred D., the obvious pleasant *outer* form of the person was not in keeping with the hidden, distressed *inner* form. And yet it is this hidden inner form, this important self-image, which shapes your destiny.

How is this self-image formed? how is it revealed?

Chapter 3

HOW YOU DEVELOP YOUR SELF-IMAGE

You are unique. Like nobody else on earth. How did you get that way?

Individuation is not just a matter of chromosomes and genes, important as heredity may be. Personality—that unique constellation of all the factors that make up the recognizable you—is an on-going attainment, beginning in infancy and continuing throughout life.

Suddenly one day a child, usually around two-and-a-half years of age, says *I* instead of *me*. In saying "I go" instead of "me go," he is verbalizing his recognition that he is the *subject* rather than the *object* of the verb. He has become the doer, the initiator. He has found a new power. Unconsciously, he has found his symbolic being—the *I*, which can be said to represent the *decisive self*. Psychologists are aware that this sense of himself, his *I*, affects the way he will organize and assign meaning to all his future experiences. His perceptions will be oriented toward protecting and defending this ultimate value: he will perceive and screen things through his own evaluation of his self-image.

So valuable is this concept that treatment for mentally ill persons has in many instances been considered successful when the patient finds courage to use the first person *I* followed by an active verb and direct object—i.e., "I see the house." Such direct communication appears to be a positive indicator of mental health.

Through small successes a healthy self-concept develops. A flawed, defective self-image develops gradually through a sequence of failures or lack of independence which convinces an individual that his choices for good development are few, or impossible of attainment.

Consider these two contrasting learning situations:

Jimmy, age 5, is dressing to go to kindergarten. He is working on his shoe laces. After much laborious effort, cheeks flushed and eyes triumphant, he stands up—both shoes are tied with such loose, precarious knots that they are ready to fall open with the slightest movement! His mother smiles and says, "That's great—much better than yesterday. See, if you pull this lace like this, and the other this way, you can get them both nice and tight." Jimmy gets his jacket and struggles to get into it. His mother pretends to be picking up the newspapers and lets him win the battle with a recalcitrant zipper. Then she says, "Look at you—dressed already! And you did it all by yourself." Later that evening Jimmy rushes to meet his father, yelling, "Dad, I dressed all by myself today—tied my own shoelaces better and everything!" Dad tousles his hair and says, "I'm glad you like to learn. One of these days you'll be teaching Betty (his younger sister) how it's done."

A cooperative attitude is growing in this child.

He knows his parents love him for what he is and that they find pleasure in his small successes. He is apt to become self-confident, self-reliant. For what happens objectively to a person is subjectively and privately evaluated and assimilated. From these learning situations come the feelings which permeate the concept of the self. What happens to a person is important, but what he feels about what happens is even more significant.

How different is Jimmy's case from that of Alice, who is of the same age. Alice is late again for school. She is trying to button her dress. She runs out of buttonholes, with two more buttons to do. Her mother is in a hurry; she brushes Alice's hands aside and rebuttons swiftly and correctly. Alice is hurried into her coat. The child's hands get caught in the armholes, and her mother must help her get into the coat.

Alice's mother spends a lot of time helping her out of such difficulties. Alice never seems to be able to keep up with her mother, her classmates or anyone else. The desire to *count* which each of us has is not thwarted even in Alice's case; she may view her helplessness as possessing definite advantages. Her disabilities offer her some compensation, for she is seldom ignored for long. She still counts. In her "private logic" Alice has found a helpless self-image which offers her some potential for satisfaction.

Each person must have some measure of individual success, or participate in his own self-indictment. The establishment of the self-image operates on three levels simultaneously: the physical, mental, and emotional. Being healthy or sick, short or tall, black or white, bright or dull—each quality is integrated into the total picture of the self at a particular point in time. We learn to evaluate such qualities on a private plus or minus basis. Cultural and intellectual images of what it means to be male or female in a particular society are likewise established. Girls may be doted upon in one family, for instance, while a boy is only tolerated; just the opposite may be true in another home. And what happens to the individual in the community at large affects the self-concept further.

The self-concept does not originate simply through feedback, however; each individual learns to look for and select, unconsciously, each event which reinforces the picture he is building of himself. We wish to succeed in establishing an identity that is powerful enough to be recognized. "If I can't be good at being good, I'll be good at being bad," expresses a need for achievement, negative though it may be. Interpretation of the self may be realistic or mere fantasy to the outside observer, but to *you*, this self you perceive is equated with truth.

Psychotherapy is less than eighty years old. As yet there appears to be no one general theory or uniformity of technique for healing the mentally or emotionally ill. However, there is basic agreement among behavioral scientists that the fundamental cause of personality damage is a poor self-image. Healing begins when the patient's private assessment of his worth improves. As he achieves an acceptable self-image, despair lessens and inner and outer harmony may be restored. No matter how old we are, an unconscious scrutiny of the developing self is maintained. We may, in fact, become set in our ways as we age because we choose rigidly to reinforce our set identity as we view it.

The written capital letter *I*, symbolic of the person himself, stands out uniquely from the rest of the handwriting as vividly as you stand out from the rest of mankind. The *I*, standing alone, represents the core of the conscious self.

Graphologically, the pp*I* is like a magnifying glass which presents the writer's vulnerabilities and assets. The inner view is changeable—it may run the gamut from healthy self-esteem to personal despair during the hours of a single day. Much of this will be reflected on paper. The fixation or flexibility of the personality will be indicated, and whatever is indicated seems real to the writer at the time of writing. The basic personality, however, remains recognizable.

Combined with other letters into words (Idaho, Interesting people, etc.,) the *I* has a common value quite different from the importance attained when used alone. An examination of the handwriting in Figure 4 containing the *I* used both as a personal pronoun and as a common capital letter, shows a significant number of graphological differences:

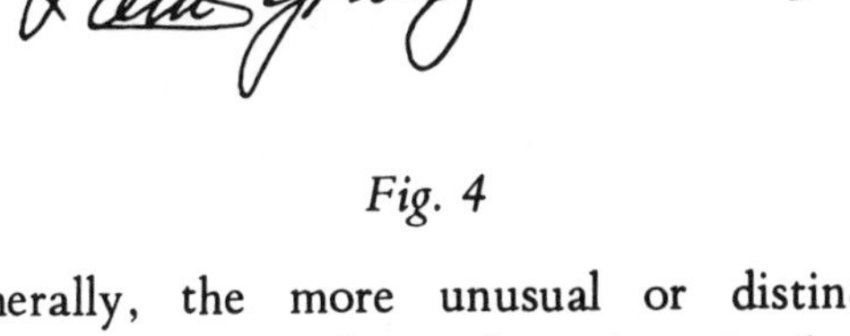

Fig. 4

Generally, the more unusual or distinctive the personality, the more distinctly unique is the personal pronoun compared to the capital letter *I* written by the same individual. Yet, no matter how slight the variations, if they are consistently maintained, each gives evidence of the personality. Differences appear to be rooted in private symbolic meaning. To the trained analyst, emotional involvement beyond the ordinary is evident when great disparities exist between the two.

The personal pronoun should be interpreted through comparison and relationships with other letters within the handwriting. Strictly speaking, it cannot be evaluated alone; like the self, the ego symbol exists and finds its identity in its relation to the environment. Nevertheless, the pp*I* can offer valuable clues to the inner personality even without such comparison, if that dire necessity arises, for basic graphological values and indicators can be reliably assigned to it.

The copybook, or school-model of the written capital *I* is standard for teaching. Both Palmer and Zaner-Bloser methods have been taught over a period of years, and these curved forms, with only slight modification, are still used in America, although some private schools prefer to teach the more distinctive print-script.

The stereotyped form starts slightly below or at the baseline, sweeps leftward into a steep loop about twice the height of the middle zone letters, (such as a, e, i, o, u, m, n, r, s, etc.) which have no extensions.[1] The *I* then descends into a curve down to the baseline and continues to the left in an arc about as long as the height of the

[1] Zones in writing are discussed in Chapter eight.

upper part. Here the curve stops, then reverses to the right
in an angle parallel to the baseline, ending a shade past the
upper loop's base.

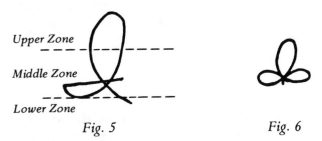

Upper Zone

Middle Zone

Lower Zone

Fig. 5   Fig. 6

Above are two ego symbols—Figure 5 a copybook or
school model—Figure 6, an unusually formed pp*I*
belonging to a fifteen-year-old girl.

Changing the copybook style of your written *I* is an
indication of individuality. Janet's decorative ego symbol
reflects her self-image:

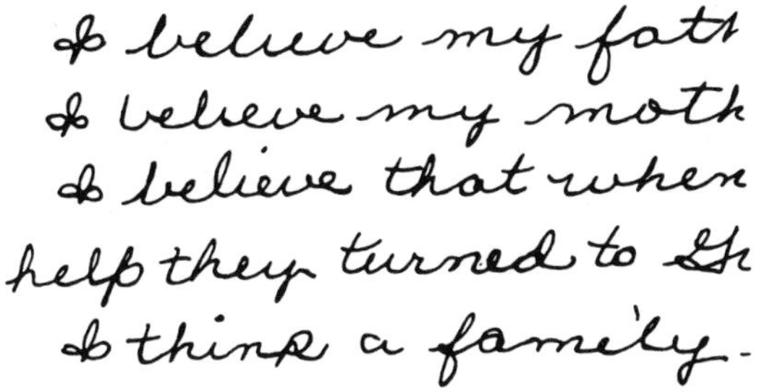

I believe my fath
I believe my moth
I believe that when
help they turned to th
I think a family.

Fig. 7

Janet is an only child, born late in her parents'
marriage and the center of their lives. She is a charming

person who loves flowery, frilly things, and her room is awash with stuffed animals and dolls.

Emphasis is put in the middle zone area of social concerns: the writer is well aware of her peer group. The pp*I* is curved, yet tightly written, showing yielding qualities mixed with tension: Janet has a difficult time facing stress such as school exams.

Two pillow-like appendages support and almost embrace the center loop. Janet requires the brace of both parents, as her small ego symbol suggests: whenever possible, her mother waits for her and drives her home from junior high school. Janet has her parents in her service; still, she has very little independence. It is interesting to note that her written *I* somewhat resembles a flower: flowers need careful tending, as does this young lady.

Chapter 4

THE UNITY OF THE SELF-IMAGE

Even to the amateur with an untrained eye, a study of the handwriting samples on pages 32 and 33 reveals distinct contrasts. Figure 8 conveys a quality of wholeness, of unity. The spacing is even and balanced, the writing flows easily with a slight rightward slant, there is a suggestion of harmony in the entire finely framed script with its comfortable margins. Figure 9, on the other hand, presents a message of confusion and instability: the baseline rises and falls, the writing is erratically spaced, shapes are distorted, the margins are uneven.

Handwriting is unified action on paper. Just as the personality expresses aspects of fragmentation or wholeness, a person's writing movement conveys to the analyst such elements as solidity, cohesiveness, harmony, flexibility—or their opposites: dispersement, rigidity, disparity, which are disturbing to the total unity.

The man who wrote Figure 9 is thirty-nine years old,

---

[1] Portions of this chapter were adapted by permission from an article, "The Unity of the Self-Image," by Jane Nugent Green, published in *The Individual Psychologist*, Volume 7, No. 1, 1970.

April 1

Dear Anne,

It's time to take your snow tires off —
April Fool! I do remember very vividly
when Mary was a baby the great thirty-inch
snow that bombarded us on March 28th.
It was so bad that John couldn't even get to
Mercy Hospital which was only three blocks away.

The perfect place for weather is Guadalajara,
Mexico. We stopped there for a few days on
our way back from Puerto Vallarta. I succumbed
to one of those beach gimmicks, a twelve-
minute parachute ride over the beautiful bay.
So now I'm called the "flying grandmother."

Incidentally, thanks for your Caribbean card.

Love,

Barbara

Fig. 8

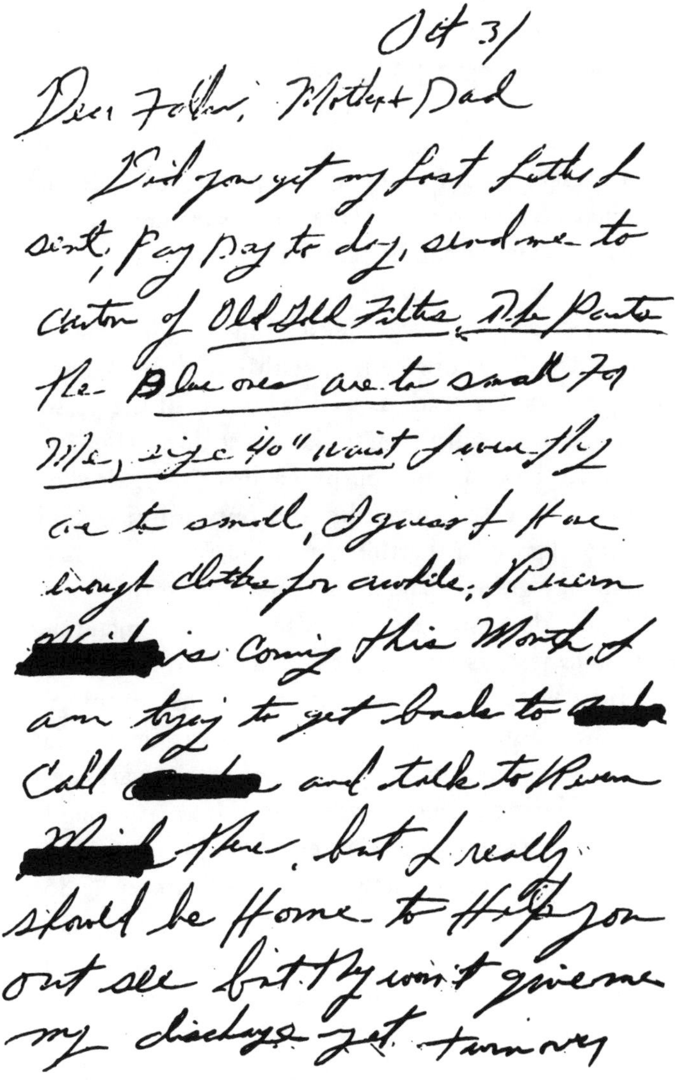

Oct 3/

Dear Father, Mother + Dad

Did you get my last letter I
sent, Pay Day to day, send me to
Center of Old Gold Filter, The Pants
the Blue ones are to small for
Me, size 40" waist of even they
are to small, I guess I Have
enough clothes for awhile; Reven
▮▮▮▮ is coming this Month, I
am trying to get back to ▮▮▮
Call ▮▮▮▮ and talk to Reven
▮▮▮ there, but I really
should be Home to Help you
out see but they won't give me
my discharge yet   turn over

Fig. 9

a diagnosed schizophrenic in a state hospital. Note that he has formed his ego symbol in five different ways. *This patient has conflicting perceptions of himself.* Lower-zone emphasis, distorted angles and displaced pressure (to be discussed later) contribute to the picture of a disturbed individual whose ego symbols reflect his trauma.

The previous chapter dealt with the uniqueness of the human being, his apartness and sense of self—a very necessary aspect of human development. This chapter is concerned with *belongingness,* with interdependence—the relating to what is inside as well as outside of the person in the world of reality where he must live. Human life appears to have a dual purpose: first, to maintain the integrity of the self, inwardly and outwardly; second, to develop and grow in the ability to cooperate.

An integrated person is one not torn apart by conflicting desires: he trusts his ability to maintain an inner sameness as he behaves in a fashion which is in keeping with his interior self. The disintegrated personality, however, due to his very lack of inner balance, is inclined to develop behavior which appears on the surface to be incongruous with reality. He may swing from one extreme to another in an effort to maintain an inner harmony which he instinctively wants. Whatever he does is expressive of his private view of himself, built upon each previous encounter with others, reinforcing his private self-image, the total unity for which he is striving.

This behavior may not be what others desire for him or expect of him, but will be what he chooses for himself, consistent with his internal view of himself. A high school counselor, discussing a student with a high I.Q., but no apparent motivation for "good" grades, said, "Arvin may, in fact, be achieving exactly what he wants, even if it is not what we want."

In other words, even behavior which is destructive and labelled neurotic makes good sense when viewed from the eyes of the person using that particular action to maintain his self-identity. If a thief believes himself to be clever only in stealing, he will resist efforts to curtail his stealing. If a girl believes she can be attractive only by promiscuous behavior, she will continue her activities and resist curtailment of them. If a child believes himself to be valuable only so long as he is noticed, he will make a nuisance of himself in public. When the observer detects this self-image and understands it, a consistency will be found which explains what, on the surface, may appear out of character or detrimental to the individual.

Therefore, it is not the acts themselves which need to be understood so much as the person standing behind each bit of behavior labelled good or bad. Understanding the self-image is the task of each person who wishes to help himself or another find successful ways of coping with life's problems. Until the self-concept is known, the true goals of a person cannot be understood. His acts will be evident but not intelligible. Although they may make perfect sense to the person performing them, the private rationale may, or may not, be in accord with common sense.

We act as we feel ourselves to be. Work with seventeen-year-old Bill dramatized these words.

One morning the handwriting analyst received a telephone call from the personnel director of a public utilities company which participated in the city's high school Work Experience Program, a part-time school, part-time job project. The personnel director was a student of graphology.

"Have you ever seen a handwriting with a small, lower-case *i* written as a personal pronoun?" she asked.

While it is rare to see an adult with so unusual an ego symbol, grade-school children sometimes write in this fashion. The analyst had seen the personal pronoun of the killer named "Zodiac", an anonymous terrorist who had killed a number of women. He had two ego symbols in his handwriting—one an overblown, grossly inflated capital, the other a miniscule and rigid dotted *i*. The killer's ego-shrinking was reflected in his tiny, "baby" *i*, at psychic war with his vanity and desire for esteem—represented by his other self, the outsized, grandiose *I*. Viewing himself as a non-entity, a powerless nobody, he nevertheless braced himself for passionate and determined hostility acted out against the enemy he saw women to be. Both deeply pressured *I*'s represented an aberrant self-image.

The personnel director was concerned about Bill, a native American boy. He had been judged to have good potential and a high-average intelligence, and at first had seemed to be making a real effort in his work. However, after a month with the company, Bill had begun to have periods of such withdrawal and moodiness that the director became worried about him.

Limited courage and self-confidence was immediately

visible in Bill's handwriting. His blotchy writing and tiny *i* indicated tension and uncertainty; his ego symbol was weakly curved and written with little pressure. Obviously the writer did not dare view himself as worthy of a normal capital *I*.

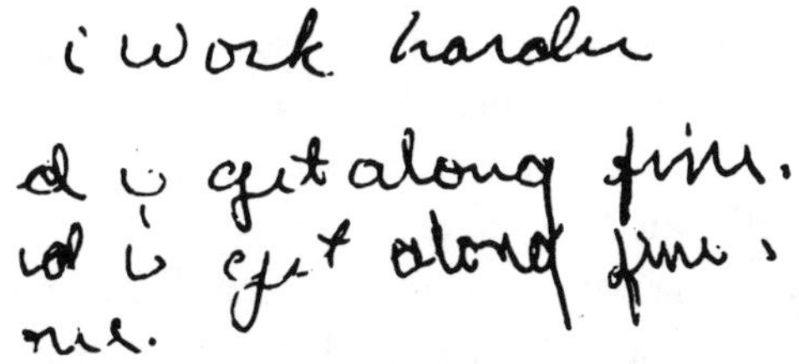

Fig. 10

When the handwriting analyst met Bill, she found him to be well-mannered, but extremely reticent. Outside of a few monosyllables, he managed only to mutter, "I knew before I even came here I wouldn't make it." Later, his words poured out.

"People keep bugging me," he blurted. "I can't do what they want. I just want to fix cars, but my mom keeps nagging me. She want me to go to college and be somebody. I know I can't make it. She says anybody can make it. But I can't. I can't even read good. And I hate school and all that." Bill's shoulders sagged and he bent his head. "That's why I first started blowing grass, it makes me feel better about myself."

He was the youngest of eight children and, although pampered, he viewed himself as a non-entity compared to his schoolmates.

A person becomes anxious if he is prevented from giving expression to what he considers his real personality. Although he may give obedience to a situation and pretend for a time that all is well, (as Bill did when he first started his job) it appears that the individual can fake it only for so long; his tolerance for disunity, or imbalance, is limited and the truth will out. It may be said then that the present is based upon that which has gone before. We repeat the patterns which have proved workable to us in the past. We remain with our feet squarely anchored in the self; trying to change behavior without understanding the self-concept is like putting a hat on a donkey and expecting it to act like a man.

Bill suffered from a preconceived expectation of failure, even in his part-time job, as attested by his words, "I knew even before I came that I wouldn't make it."

The person who anticipates certain results will act as if they are, in fact, in existence. A child who is sure nobody wants him will ultimately act as though nobody does, and his feeling of unworthiness is apt to make such dislike a fact, in spite of potentially favorable circumstances. He will try and try again and again to harmonize his interior feelings of being worthless with the outward situation.

An overly sensitive adult who meets a group of outsiders whom he considers his superiors (or inferiors) will find what he expects to find. Because he generalizes on the subject ("I am inferior" or "I am superior") he will interpret specific circumstances to suit his preconceived evaluation.

Private interpretation gives both credibility and predictability to an individual's overt performance. He will cling to behavior which to him is understandable and connected with the unity and consistency of the self as he sees it. In solving his problems, he will incorporate the principles of balance and inner order to maintain himself in a unified fashion.

Just as the outer self expresses itself through physical movements, so the private self builds its own specific behavior patterns through generalities. A well-adjusted person may be said to be an individual who can maintain a sense of balance within himself and still be in harmony with the society around him. Thus a criminal may be well-adjusted in a particular criminal society; he may, in fact, be an acknowledged leader. The places he chooses for his leadership will be the environment where he feels he has the most chance of succeeding. His behavior is consequently not a *disorder* so much as an attempt to maintain order within the personality: its expression is appropriate to the surroundings, as the person subjectively interprets them. The integrity of the personality means that the person will behave as he thinks he is able to behave under the circumstances.

Our modern vocabulary reflects this consciousness of balance and imbalance. For example, such an expression as "shook-up" is used negatively and emphasized fragmentation; "up-right", on the other hand, implies stability. The word "up-tight" carries this concept to extreme, expressing a balance maintained with rigidity, which connotes a certain anxiety on the part of the up-tight one: he fears loss of balance.

Again, in Bill's case, we find also the lack of harmony which results from confusion of goals. He wants to be a mechanic, his mother wants him to go to college, the school wants him to succeed at the utilities company. All this disunity is "bugging" him.

To be alive is to act and have goals. A striving for unity and balance within the self is a part of a person's *inner* goals. A liking for problem-solving appears to be part of the healthy human need to expand and develop *outer* goals.

A person's inner evaluation of himself triggers such outer goal manifestation. Each human marches to the refrain of "I seek myself." Answers to this problem torment (as with Bill) or delight. But they cannot be ignored. Crawling out of a playpen or escaping from a highchair keeps company with man's highly complicated efforts to land on the moon. Mankind wishes to enlarge its horizons and goals, just as the toddler who, having once escaped limiting boundaries, will try it again—and again.

The striving for unified inner and outer achievement is consistent. Self-evaluation gives a person certain standards which he uses to judge himself and his role in life; the possibilities he sees for himself appear harmonious to him, be they conventional, unconventional or even anti-social to others. To say that an individual is inconsistent is a contradiction, for while the environment may change, under normal conditions a person is consistently himself.

And so the struggle to achieve that beauty which is

unity and harmony within the self goes on, no matter how contradictory or irrational its manifestation may seem from the outside.

But there is a clue to the truth: the handwriting, reflecting—like the samples at the beginning of this chapter—the writer's state of fragmentation or his achievement of wholeness. And the ego symbol, the personal pronoun *I*, epitomizes the *heart of the matter*.

Chapter 5

YOUR ATTITUDE

I cannot be separated from *they*. Each person lives with and among people, and how well he gets along with others depends on his views of himself and of his own capacities.

A person may be conforming, yielding—one who would rather switch than fight. Or he may be self-reliant and independent, counting little on others. This independence may go even further and become the expression of a defiant personality, or one which accedes to others only after due deliberation and with his own best interests in mind.

In both work and play (and certainly in the choice of a marriage partner) people-relatedness is of primary importance. Happy is the research scientist who enjoys working alone, whose need for other people is minimal. But put this same man in a sales job where he must constantly deal with other people, and you are apt to have a very unhappy person whose inner equilibrium is constantly under strain.

Handwriting analysis has an appeal for hard-pressed businessmen who need help in employment screening, particularly for out-of-town applicants. Graphological evaluation is time-consuming only for the analyst: employment forms may simply ask a prospective employee to give a written evaluation concerning how he can best contribute to the continued growth of the company and how the company can provide for the writer's personal occupational satisfaction.

Graphological interpretation includes the over-view form level impression, millimeter measurements of various letter elements, use of a protractor for slant measurements, and mathematical assessment of other graphological factors. To evaluate around forty qualities, over one hundred fifty calculations may be made. The gestalt[1] method is used, not single "trait" characteristics. As in all professional systems, an ultimate value judgment must be given.

Does the good-looking handwriting win the best jobs? Not necessarily. Highly competitive selling, for example, takes an aggressive personality which often does not fit well with the easy-going writer.

Mr. A's handwriting in Figure 11 is large, legible and as attractive as he is. Twenty-three years of age, he was hired after his first interview for a highly competitive selling job with a chemical firm. Confident and dynamic appearing, he was a recent graduate from a sales training institute, had achieved top grades and appeared to be a natural for selling.

[1] Gestalt: Pattern or configuration which implies that the whole is not analyzable into separate parts but is an integration. Specific properties cannot be derived simply from the summation of its component parts. Graphologically, the whole is a sum greater than its parts.

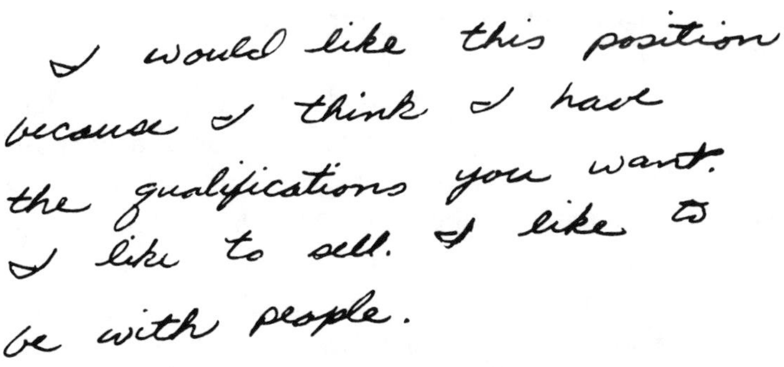

I would like this position because I think I have the qualifications you want. I like to sell. I like to be with people.

Fig. 11

As a follow-up, his firm asked for a graphological evaluation. According to the consultant's file, the following memo was sent to management:

Advise management that this young man is incapable, for the time being, of performing according to expectations: unable to handle the fast response, give and take, maneuvering the buyer, creating interesting points to consider, building strategic needs in the buyers' mind for the product. Rather, he is dependent, not aggressive, but if he could make progress on his likeable personality, then he should be nurtured slowly.

However, management was convinced that Mr. A. would make the grade. They gave him two weeks' intensive training, then sent him out on his own in a new territory.

He lasted three days.

Competing with others in a tough territory was neither a challenge nor an opportunity to him, as it would have been for the hard-core salesman. Graphological interpretation had shown that Mr. A. was too dependent on others to enjoy aggressive competition and constant change. It was suggested that he would do well in a behind-the-counter selling job. This he is now doing, successfully.

Mr. A's pp*I* indicates a great deal about his emotional and pliable personality: it is forward-slanted and reclined. His charm and outgoing manner are assets to him when he does not have to compete to win.

Clues to your social and emotional inclinations are found in the slant of the written *I*, as well as other letters. The copybook *I* is approximately 45-55 degrees to the

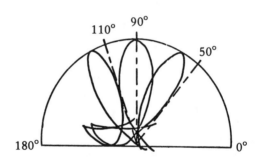

Fig. 12

right, measured by the angle formed by the downstroke with the baseline. This slant is a natural one, following the average, righthand motion in handwriting. It leans in the direction of the righthand margin.

This slant is considered symptomatic of the outgoing individual, in part because all graphic movement to the right is considered future- or goal-oriented. Symbolically as well as actually, this is where the writer is headed as he progresses across the page.

Leftward movement, on the other hand, implies regression toward the past. That is where you have been on the writing page. We seem to have unconscious knowledge, in western culture, of such relationships to forward and backward direction.

Writing which moves to the right appears to be least stressful or resistant to forward progression. Of course, slant may be modified considerably if you are left-handed, hold your pen in an unusual manner, or change the angle of the paper. However, artificial slant cannot be maintained for long periods.

Your emotional attitude toward your social environment is expressed in great measure through slant: you may feel emotionally free to forge easily ahead (rightward slanted writing), or you may control your reactions (vertical slant) or you may repress any forward movement (backhand slant).

In other words, you may choose to meet the environment easily, shown by forward-moving motion, or you may resist, shown by slant inclined to the left. Backhand writing of the ppl indicates a certain withdrawal from the situation—you are inclined to size things up before committing yourself.

I go to school in

Fig. 13

If you are inclined to express your feelings openly, chances are that you will write with a rightward slant.

I knew several people

Fig. 14

If you are poised and controlled by judgment rather than emotions, your *I* may be vertical.

If I could change

Fig. 15

If you are inclined to put brakes on your emotions, then your writing usually will show indications toward the left.

I think I could

Fig. 16

Changes in the slant of the I within the same text imply changes in emotion concerning the self.

The Consenting You

A consistent and moderate slant is a visual manifestation of control and balance. Ease in slanting your writing evenly forward indicates ease in rhythmically moving toward others. Graphologically, you are able to do this because you maintain a balance between the outgoing, upward stroke and the in-gathering, downward stroke.

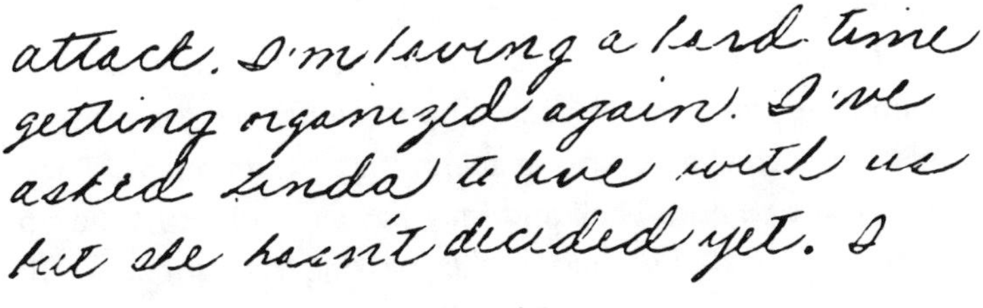

Fig. 17

Release is part of the *upward* motion; *control* is emphasized in a *down*ward motion, as it is when you reach upward or down.

Flexor muscles make the downstrokes which go toward the *self.* Extensor muscles of the hand push the stroke *away* from the writer. Psychological interpretation suggests that an even, rightward-moving slant indicates "obedience" to moving in a taught manner along the writing page. Moderation is suggested through even control of the downstroke which gives the writing its rhythm, or "beat." The importance of controlling the handwriting through an even downstroke is known by teachers of the early grades who understand the principles of writing. Emphasis should be placed on starting each printed letter at the top rather than the bottom. The downstroke in handwriting is naturally controlled: going down makes swinging up easier for the child. Doing it backwards is awkward; yet immature or left-handed children may begin printing from the bottom rather than from the top of each letter. This habit is hard to break; it lessens the good appearance and speed of printing, and the child is apt to become discouraged and blame himself.

Right-slanted *I* writers usually act promptly or even on impulse; their nature insists upon emotional expression, and they often have strong feelings at the moment. They don't want to hold back and may have a tendency to jump to conclusions. The more the writing slants below 40 degrees rightward, the more over-reaction may be expected.

Mr. A's 30 degree slanted pp*I* in Figure 11 implies a yielding self-concept. Dependence upon others and emotionality play a large part in his life.

The Dissenting You

While going outward away from the self is equated with centrifugal movement, going inward toward the self is equated graphologically with centrepital or leftward movement.

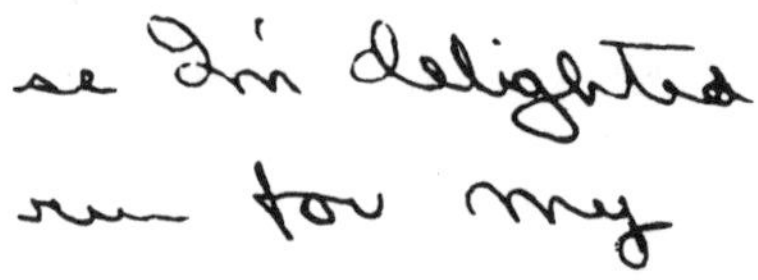

Fig. 18

Left-tending *I*'s are not easily written by the right

hand: they are, therefore, more artificially executed unless the writer is actually left-handed. The right-handed writer is literally bending backward. By negating forward movement, the vertical or backhand pp*I* implies some defiance toward going ahead emotionally toward others.

If you are such a writer, you may have an inner reserve even though on the surface you appear socially at ease. However, since your self-esteem is guarded through privacy, your tendency toward formality or structured activity may say "hands off." Well-executed writing of this type is equated with a somewhat practiced behavior and is always more contrived than a rightward writing.

Backhand writing is common among teenagers reluctant to be committed to things not of their own choosing. Sometimes such attitudes may go beyond reserve, as they seek to find their own identity. Withdrawal from commonly accepted values may cause defiance as conventional social attitudes are discarded.

Here are examples of backhand *I*'s and a few facts about the writers, all of whom are right-handed:

Fig. 19

The teenager who wrote Figure 19 is seeking her own identity. She is self-protective and resents adults.

Fig. 20

The writer of Figure 20 is a talented homemaker who enjoys solitude. She likes traditional things and is oriented toward the past.

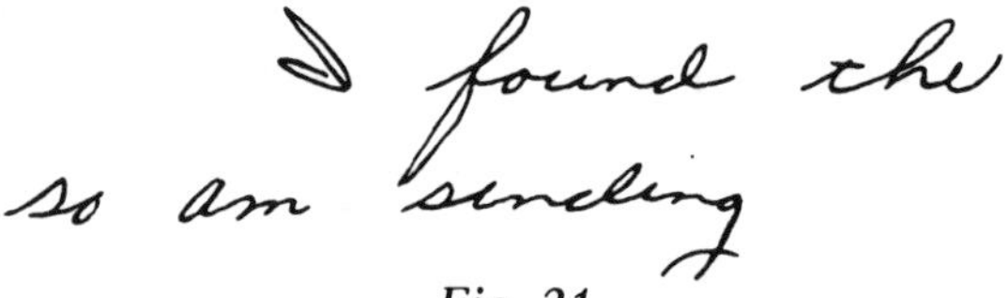

I found the
so am sending

Fig. 21

The woman who wrote Figure 21 has an active social life but relates easily to others only on a superficial level. Note the differences in writing slant.

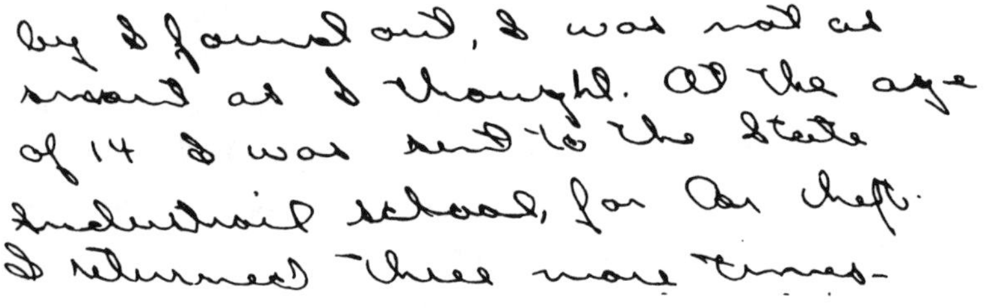

Fig. 22

The writer of Figure 22 is a prisoner who has long been at odds with others. Left-tending strokes emphasize his defensiveness.

The Centered You

The vertical *I* may be the thinking person's response to involvement. Here is an example:

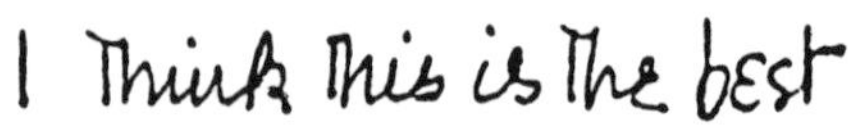

I Think this is The best

Fig. 23

By blocking out distracting emotions, this kind of individual can live more easily, retain a feeling of independence and protect his innermost feelings. The ego may thus guard itself from intimacy by taking a little time to study the situation. In actuality, it does take more time and effort to control the forward motion.

You, the vertical writer, wish to get the facts before committing yourself emotionally; therefore, you may frustrate persons who are less restrained. Nevertheless, you refrain from impulsive action and are apt to be cautious in relationships. You consider the consequences of your actions before becoming involved.

What happens when a "consenting" (rightward slant) *you* marries a "dissenting" or "centered" *you?* Very mature individuals may find their personality differences complementary and stimulating. They may get along harmoniously. But sometimes tension and frustration result, as illustrated by the couple who wrote Figures 24 and 25:[2]

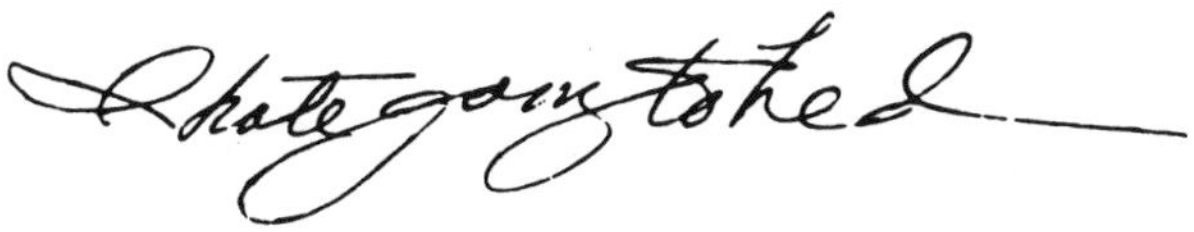

Fig. 24

This woman is gregarious, uninhibited and emotionally expressive. The household is noisy, unregulated and filled with projects and people.

[2] It must be stressed that the graphologist is not ordinarily a trained counselor. The technique of handwriting analysis may be utilized as an additional tool in professional counseling.

I'm still working away at

Fig. 25

Her husband's upright slant and small, precise script reflects his personality. He is reserved, methodical, enjoys solitary pursuits and teaching history.

Understanding their unspoken attitudes expressed through each handwriting assisted the marriage counselor in pin-pointing problems and possible resolutions.

Chapter 6

RELATIONSHIPS AND RELATION-SHAPES

"What do you think might be a problem with this patient of mine?" asked the psychologist, as he gave the graphologist the handwriting of a fifty-year-old man shown in Figure 26.

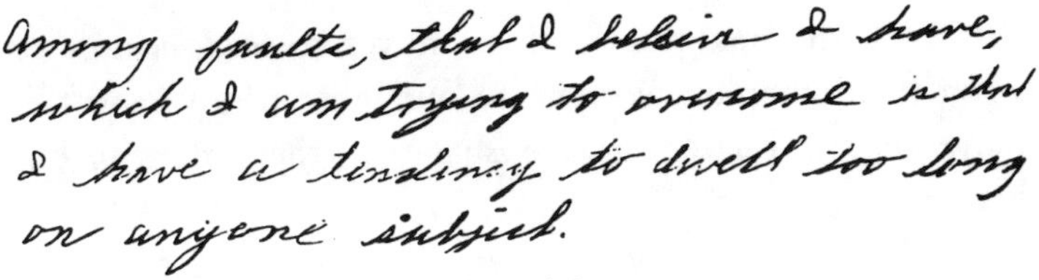

Among faults, that I believe I have, which I am trying to overcome is that I have a tendency to dwell too long on anyone subject.

Fig. 26

The graphologist was struck by the distinct difference between the angular strokes of the writer's letters and the soft, rounded ego symbol. The pp*I* held back from the rest of the forward-moving writing—it alone was left-tending. The aggression of the dynamic angles was apparent. The inner softness of the gentleman's self-image was also apparent.

The graphologist suggested that because of this inner conflict, the writer might have an excessive need to prove himself right, to the detriment of his personal relationships. A second problem might be that he would feel a need to defend himself against intimate relationships.

The psychologist agreed. The writer had been in constant conflict with his wife and children, whom he sought to dominate through rigid rules. A successful dentist, he nevertheless felt that things were going from bad to worse in both his private and professional life. In spite of an outwardly aggressive attitude, he lacked inner self-confidence, due to a faulty self-concept. He had been orphaned at an early age and was raised by uncompromising relatives who made him feel unwanted much of his life. Inner feelings of helplessness dominated him.

Like this man, each of us moves *toward, against* or *away* from people according to our inner needs. And this movement is related to the shape of the letters in our handwriting.

All letters are formed by curved or straight strokes. As part of expressive motion, the curved stroke is flexible—the straight stroke is inflexible. Which strokes you emphasize in your writing emphasizes your inner needs in relating to others.

The ordinary copybook *I* combines both flexible and inflexible strokes in a total well-balanced shape. How you modify this basic shape offers clues to your relationship with others. Are your relationships fundamentally flexible and yielding? Or are they firm and inflexible? Are these positive or negative factors in your life?

Let us examine the most common writing strokes:

Curved strokes are the easiest and most rhythmical to make. They are called *garlands* because they form a running stroke which is open at the top, similar to a hanging garland or a curved cup. Because they are so naturally and easily made, garlands emphasize lack of stress, lack of friction, and accommodation to others. Not only connections between letters may be curved this way, but m's and n's may be written in u-shapes, rather than in copybook fashion.

The straight handwriting stroke is termed an *angle*. Consistent use of the angle in writing forms most often signifies determination, plus a certain amount of conflict. The writer is apt to be careful, methodical and analytical.

A third stroke is termed an *arcade*. It is the opposite of the open garland, since it is covered up, a humped stroke. Writing which employs this form a great deal implies careful thinking and attention to form.

The fourth writing stroke is called a *thread*, since it resembles a thread. The most formless of writing, it suggests speed and impatience, since its letters are only hinted at within the structure.

If one of these strokes—the garland, angle, arcade or thread,—characterizes your writing, what does it reveal about you and your relationships with others?

Going Toward Others

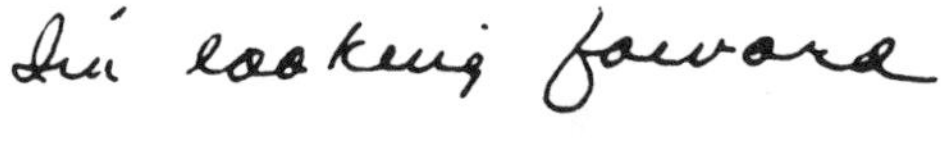

Fig. 27

In relating to others, the garland writer such as the one in Figure 27 is sociable, tolerant, sympathetic and adaptable. (Note the u-shaped letters).

However, when an unusually open garland pp*l* stroke is found, it suggests an unusual receptivity toward others as well as undue influence of past experiences. These qualities may add up to being distractable. In Figures 28 and 29 we have garland writers. Both move easily toward others, but the first writer's garlands are an asset to her; the second one's are a liability.

Rounded arcade letters and curved garlands connecting each letter indicate positive factors of poise and grace which this writer brings to her life. Married to a Lieutenant Commander in the United States Navy, she is well suited to her demanding social role. Ease of communication, an eye for detail and a logical mind are apparent in the well-spaced, finely executed letters. Her generosity is shown by garland upswings at the end of words. However, the writer is not as easily swayed as she might socially appear: control is shown by even margins

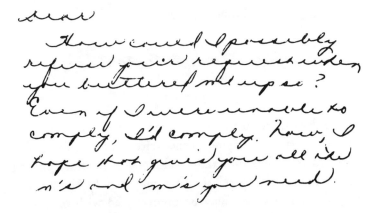

Fig. 28

and writing alignment. The cup-like garland stroke at the end of her pp*I* is emphasized by the extra pressure she gives it. The writer moves toward others and is at home with them.

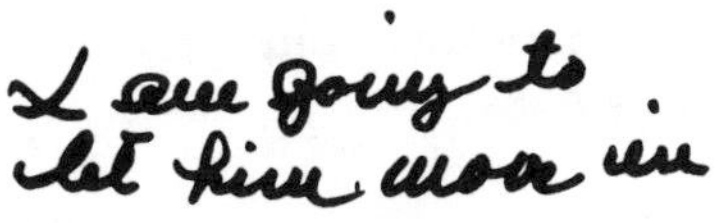

Fig. 29

The self-image of the overly-garland pp*I* in Figure 29 is one of defeat and over-reaction which causes emotional exhaustion. She has taken the path of least resistance at times and is raising an illegitimate daughter. Note the cup-shaped *I*, indicating the writer's susceptibility to the past and to the influence of others.

Going Against Others

Fig. 30

Substituting angles for curved writing may be more psychologically gratifying to the writer who sees himself as opposed to others or standing alone. An uncompromising rather than yielding relationship may signify the angular writer. Such a writer may be preoccupied with order and precision. He does not take the easy way. He may have a need for getting down to essentials and cutting through extraneous details. Buttressed angles such as the ones in Figure 30 imply a need to fortify the position of the writer.

An angular pp*I* is indicative in many instances of the writer's perception of structure and form. Engineers, architects, mathematicians and craftsmen often use a severely angular pp*I*:

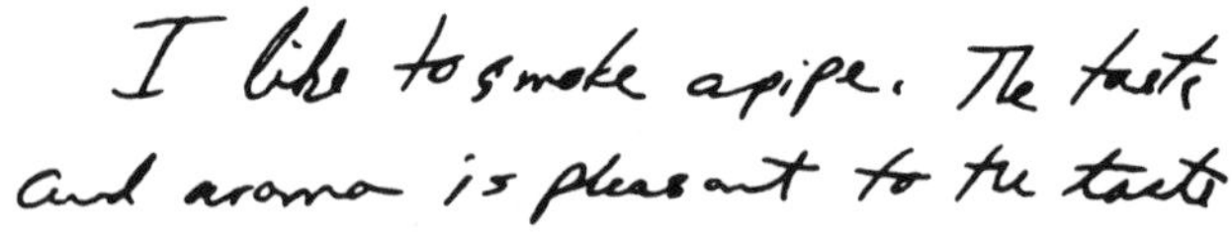

Fig. 31

The engineer who wrote Figure 31 is highly successful in his job which involves a great deal of painstaking detail work. He insists upon meticulous craftsmanship. His printed *I* implies independence and the need to do things in an orderly fashion.

If your *I* is angular, the extra care involved in this form may offer reassurance that you are preserving your identity as well as carrying out your goals. To the angular writer, "reality" is apt to involve a firm commitment to decisions. Relationships are apt to be more rigid than those of the writer with a softly curved pp*I*. The self-image of the angular writer implies purpose. Going against others and achieving independence involves inflexible determination.

Going Away From Others

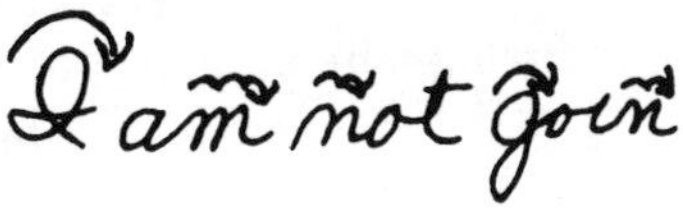

Fig. 32

The conventional copybook *I* is predominantly arcade. This stroke is closed at the top and open downward (like copybook m, n). It is an inverted cup, arching and enclosing. Arcades result from controlled contraction movements of the pen, in contrast to the open release motion of the garland.

The arcade has a vault effect. The specific inner experience of the ego which this form conveys is protective. It emphasizes safeguards against intimacy, a need for covering up, possibly some desire for privacy or concealment. Symbolically, the arcade offers covering strokes more carefully formed than the garland and less rigid than the angle. The arcade is a kind of compromise. It is less time-consuming to make than the angle, more time-consuming than the garland. Psychologically, the arcade may be thought to say: "I am taking time for self-regulation before facing the world, before relating to others from my protected position."

The garland has been compared to an open hand, the angle to a fist, the arcade to a glove which covers and smooths. The *I* which is more arcade than copybook suggests the need to protect the self from intimacy. Because the arcade implies going away from others and concern for the self, it may be compared to a shell placed around the ego for protection and support. The writer is most at home in a setting which he makes for himself. The writer of the arcade *I* is not open for easy inspection.

Fig. 33

Figure 33 shows the arcade ego symbol of a bright and capable lady executive who enjoys a challenge but prefers a structured situation in which to work. She is a sensitive person who does not easily reveal her innermost feelings. She prefers to set her own goals.

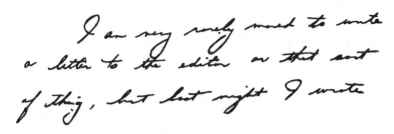

Fig. 34

If your pp*I* is arcade and your writing of creative form level, (to be discussed later) you are likely to have artistic inclinations, to enjoy beautiful things in the arts field and to respect tradition, social form and good manners. The arcade ego symbol in Figure 34, written by a young woman who is both a musician and a mathematician, reflects interest in formality, as well as in aesthetical and philosophical matters. Its simplification shows her independence.

Staying In The Middle

The arcade pp*I* in Figure 34 is accompanied by well articulated thread writing of high form level. Thread writing, characterized by indistinct, wavy or thread-like strokes, is rapid writing in which garlands, angles and arcades are joined together and trail off into a single line without forming a very distinguishable pattern.

Thread writing is largely shapeless, unconventional, and not easy to read. Thread writing which is slow appears contradictory—it is usually of low form level.

The psychological essence of thread connectives appears to be an unwillingness to being categorized. Lack of definite pattern, a desire to be in the middle and view both sides, a need to be an "individual" are usually characteristic of the thread writer. The habitual thread writer often does not enjoy close scrutiny of his motives. Many thread writers possess great charm, since they have empathy with others and awareness of coming trends: they are "tuned-in."

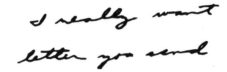

Fig. 35

The tiny thread writing of an adolescent boy is shown in Figure 35. Avoidance of communication became apparent in both his actions and his writing as he struggled through an identity crisis. When the writer achieved inner harmony, his self-confidence bloomed, as did his handwriting: it became larger and more decipherable.

Chapter 7

YOUR SELF AND SPACE

"What do you suppose made her run away?" asked the perturbed high school counselor. Beverly, the student in question, was one of the school's outstanding seniors, a beautiful girl with an estimated I.Q. of 140. She had been missing for two weeks. The counselor added, "I know she has a hippie brother, but she was always very conforming around here. And I've talked often to the parents—they're so proud of her. She seems to have made up to them for all the trouble they've had with her brother. And now, just like that, she runs away from home!"

The graphologist looked at Beverly's nicely margined, well-spaced script—shown in Figure 36—which the counselor handed her. Then at the revealing *I*. It appeared that if the writer had been as much of a conformist as the counselor thought, she would not be so apt to write her ego symbol with a simple, straight line. And if Beverly felt a great deal of self-confidence, chances were that the pp*I* would be taller. The high form level of writing indicated sensitive awareness on the writer's part. The graphologist suspected that the writer had a real yearning to stand alone, to see herself as an individual. She promised to send a detailed report within a few days.

Fig. 36

Later, the graphologist was interrupted in her careful scrutiny of Beverly's writing by the arrival of the morning mail. By coincidence, it brought her the handwriting of a forty-nine year-old man whose flamboyant ego symbol—written high, wide and handsome and with a telltale grasping hook on the end—stood in contrast to that of our missing student.

Fig. 37

Beverly's stripped-down *I* seemed to say, "I don't want things. I don't want my parents. I don't want what I've had. Just let me be free, let me be myself." Mr. K's ego symbol, shown in Figure 37, said just the opposite: "I want things. I want money. I want people. I want to be noticed. I'm clever and I can get all these things. Even this space I'm writing in belongs to me."

When Beverly was found it turned out she was living in a dingy, sub-standard rooming house and working as a waitress in a truck-stop restaurant. Many hours of counseling revealed that Beverly was indeed rebelling against her parents' wishes for her and expectations of her.

Her father, a violinist in a symphony orchestra, and her mother, a librarian who surrounded herself with books and ideas both at home and at work, needed Beverly's achievements in part to wipe out their son's failures. Beverly's running away from home and dropping out of school were a rejection of her intellectual heritage and her parents' demands. She was also bitter about her brother, whom she felt her parents had estranged. Like her brother, she wanted to show that she could stand alone and be herself.

As for Mr. K.—he was indeed the acquisitive soul. Unfortunately, his talents had been misdirected toward illegal get-rich-quick projects, the last of which misfired. He had tried to expedite the liquidation of his wealthy wife's estate by forging her signature on some checks—only to be thwarted by an equally acquisitive relative, who had his heart set on a handsome inheritance.

Both of these writers—Beverly and Mr. K.—in writing their ego symbols had used space to express integral parts of their concepts about themselves. The particular arrangement of the *I* on paper is both symbolic and expressive. Unconscious feelings toward space and its use offer clues to the writer's self-esteem, how he relates to others, what inclinations he may possess.

Just for a moment, conjure up the following mental pictures involving space, and what that space communicates:

Three persons are on a street corner waiting for a bus.

They stand apart, not speaking, a wide space between each one. What does the space say? Separateness. Isolation.

Two lovers walk down a campus path, arms entwined around each other's waists. No space there. Closeness. Intimacy.

A wild fawn lets a human come just so near—then, a flick of white tail and he leaps away. Physical distance. Safety.

A woman says, "I dislike parties, but I like to talk to people on the phone." Distance here, too. Psychological distance, and safety.

And so it is with handwriting. The page is space, and the way a writer approaches his page is symbolic of the way he approaches the world. Margins indicate space between him and the environment. Graphologically, the entire sheet of paper as well as the words upon it are a part of the symbolic environment of the written *"I."*

Your Use of Size depends upon your feelings about relating to others. Each person tends to write with a consistent letter size which takes up a certain amount of space, no matter how he was taught to write in school.

The size of the taught copybook script is around 3 millimeters in middle-letter height. People who write this size consistently are most apt to fit themselves into conventional or prevailing circumstances. Other factors being equal, adaptability and balance of mind go hand-in-hand with average size.

Larger than average handwriting is often written by those who like to make an impression. They may enjoy attention and admiration, with their force of personality gaining them followers.

Small writing may be a sign of superior intelligence and ability to concentrate. In contrast to large script, which suggests interest in a generalized overview of plans, persons or things, the tiny writing indicates a writer viewing things in detail or minutiae.

Seeing design as a whole, the human eye organizes space and size in relation to the entirety. Thus the *I* reflects the personality in part through its relationship to words preceding or following it. Just as you cannot "see" written size without comparison to other letters, you cannot notice movement without a background. Establishing the gestalt of size becomes a relative matter.

Some personal pronouns are unusually large even when the paper is small. The writer who demands so much space for his ego symbol no matter how little may be left for the rest of the writing, says something about his desire for elbow-room.

The way in which the writer utilizes handwriting space may suggest his interests. Concentrated effort to write small implies some inclination toward analyzing concepts or noting details. Many scientists, engineers, psychologists and mathematicians have small writing. On the other hand, actors, salesmen and persons enjoying being where the action is often write with a large, flourishing hand.

Your Use of Vertical Space in writing your pp*I* is related to your need for self-assurance. The capital *I* averages about 1½ to 2½ times the size of the copybook middle letters without extensions, such as a, o, e, m, n etc. The actual proportion of the ego symbol in comparison with other letters is moderate when the contrast is neither exaggerated nor minimized, as in Figure 38.

Fig. 38

Such an *I* in reasonable proportion portrays careful consideration and moderation on the part of the writer. This writer's goals are conventional; she concentrates easily on the goals she has; she visualizes herself as a realistic person. Her self-respect is based in part upon practicality.

Exaggeration in size indicates strong feelings concerning your ego. The taller you write your pp*I* the more ambitious you appear to be for activity which can enhance your ego. Extension into the heights implies desire on the writer's part for distinction. Possible vanity and a desire for recognition are part of the self-image when the ego symbol looms above other letters, as illustrated in Figure 39.

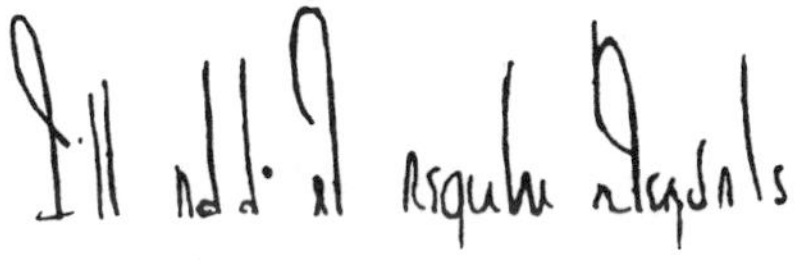

Fig. 39

When, on the other hand, you restrict the height of your *I*, the chances are that you also restrict yourself in some manner. The writer who forms his pp*I* so small that it barely pokes its head above the height of the middle letters indicates modesty and lack of self-assertion. This kind of writer does not possess pretentious attitudes. Like Beverly's pp*I*, the self-concept may be more effacing than demanding.

Extremes of ego height or ego shrinking will be discussed later. Both are aspects of the same thing: self-concern. Always, actual millimeter size is relative—the proportions between other letters and the *I*, as well as the page size, must be considered.

Like Beverly, many teenagers write with smaller than average handwriting because they are still discovering their own individuality and are not yet certain of themselves. Others will feel the necessity to write their ego symbol unusually large. However, in many cases the proportion is not as disparate as it at first glance may appear, because the middle letters are large.

Seventeen-year-old Sylvia, a go-go dancer, illustrates this point in Figure 40.

at home, ⌿

Fig. 40

Sylvia's mother is a prostitute who has never given her daughter a conventional home. Sylvia's pp*I* appears to be inflated, but the proportion of her ego symbol to the middle zone letters is not as great as it first appears. Sylvia needs lots of attention from people. She dreams of breaking into the movies some day. But, underneath, her self-image is not as confident as her actions appear.

Your Use of Horizontal Space in writing your *I* may be narrow or it may be broad. The more narrow the space is, the more constricted and compressed may be the view you hold of yourself. As usual, form level plays a large part in determining if using space broadly or narrowly is an asset or liability to you.

Narrow

In a negative sense, the writer may be inclined toward conservative or inflexible reactions. A retraced pp*I* suggests defensiveness and the rejection from consciousness of painful or disagreeable ideas, memories, feelings or impulses. The writer may be repressed and lack insight. On the positive side, creative individuals (to be discussed later) may choose to simplify their use of space and narrow their "vision" into special endeavors.

Broad

The more inflated and imaginative the writer's

self-concept, the broader the loops of the *I* may be. Such over-size, expanded ego symbols indicate as a rule an outgoing individual who may also enjoy the spotlight. Fantasizing or wishful thinking may be equated with unusually dilated loops in the pp*I*.

Your Use of Distance is in keeping with the whole gestalt of your ego-symbol. The spacing between words

Fig. 41

and between lines offers clues to the psychological-graphological unity of the self. Wide spacing between your *I* and other words expresses a concept of cautious pause when relating to others. You literally and figuratively keep your distance. In a positive sense, such wide spacing symbolizes a need for thinking before proceeding. The writer may have the capacity to be objectively critical of himself and of others. When carried to extreme, such lack of spontaneity hints at the ego's need to control. Such over-control may imply self-conscious inhibition. Careful spacing is often symptomatic of the perfectionist.

When the writer's *I* consistently crowds its neighboring words, the need for continuing association with others may be inferred. If too crowded, such needs may be expressed through impulsiveness which elbows out caution. On the positive side, the writer may have quick, instinctual responses to the needs of others.

Fig. 42

The writer of Figure 42 connects her *I* with the next word. This habit suggests that her self-concept is closely connected or related to others. She is an outgoing, gregarious person who has quick empathy with others. She is a social worker and enjoys her work.

Sometimes in the same text the pp*I* may be placed very close to words, then spaced in isolation. Such inconsistency disturbs the orderly progression of writing. Sometimes aloof, sometimes aggressive, this kind of writer may vacillate in organizational and social aspects. Such unevenness in spatial organization hints at unevenness in dealing with affairs in an orderly fashion. For example, writing which has uneven lines and bumps into the line above or below with letter extensions (such as f, g, y) suggests a writer who takes on too much at a time.

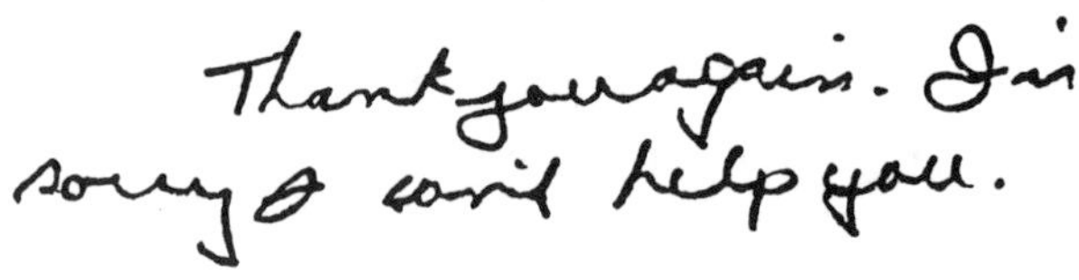

Fig. 43

The self-assurance of 23-year-old Alice fluctuates

from day to day, just as her personal pronoun changes size within a single sentence as in Figure 43. Inconsistency in dealing with others adds to her difficulty, as varying distances between words portray.

Your Sense of Organization implies a sense of direction. The ability to write in an orderly fashion appears in part to depend on the writer's ability to achieve working harmony with the physical self, the emotions and the will. You know what needs to be done—and you do it.

The graphological clue here is the baseline (where the writing rests). This baseline gives direction to the line of writing. The direction can be straight (parallel to the bottom of the page), it can be upward, or it can go down. You can best judge your writing alignment by drawing a line under the base of the small letters.

Even Line Direction

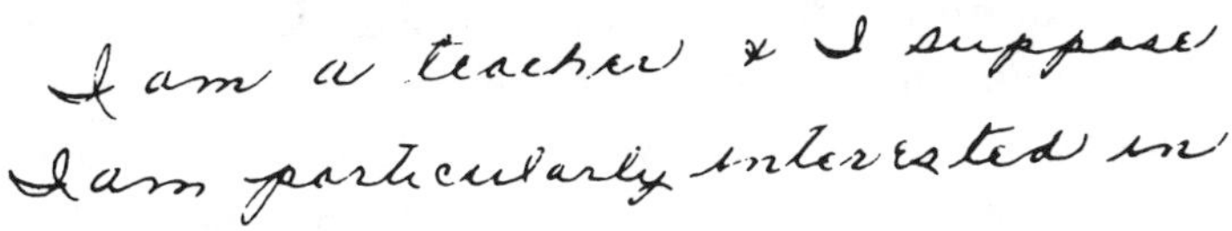

Fig. 44

Even line direction gives evidence of your sensitivity to organization and controlled actions. The *I* is placed where you want it to go in relationship to the rest of the letters. An *I* in good alignment denotes ability to organize your practical endeavors. When it is consistently and squarely placed on the baseline, your self-direction is emphasized. The straighter the writing line, the more emphasis you place in setting goals for yourself in a practical and effective manner. (Some people use rulers to enhance their straightness of line, others must use lined paper.) Fluctuation is natural, as in Figure 44, which has a spontaneous harmony.

Uneven Line Direction

Uneven line direction may indicate inconsistent judgments. In other words, you may change your mind

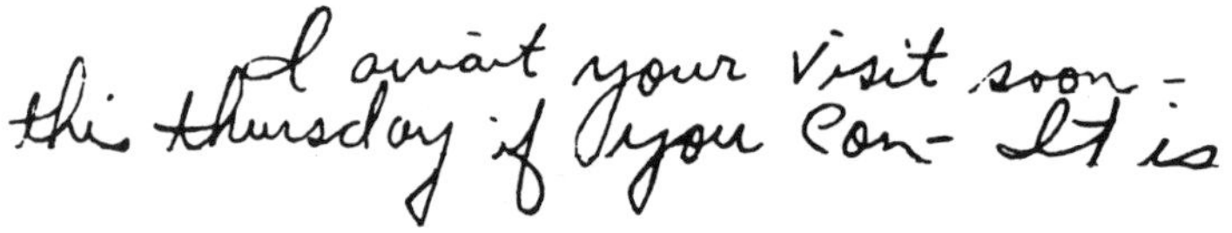

Fig. 45

numerous times concerning what needs to be done. Such inconsistency may be beneficial or harmful to the writer; for example, if you are particularly imaginative, fluctuations may merely be evidence of adaptability and creative fervor. In a negative sense, indecisiveness may lead to unproductive postponement of decisions and activity.

The writer of Figure 45 is a 38-year old man. He is a perpetual student who holds a menial blue-collar job. Ever restless, he floats from place to place. Judgment has been further impaired by barbiturate addiction. In spite of using lined paper, he cannot hold an even baseline. Indecisiveness and anxiety mark his life. Numerous other graphological factors point to a poor self-image. These will be discussed in further chapters.

Upward Rising Line Direction

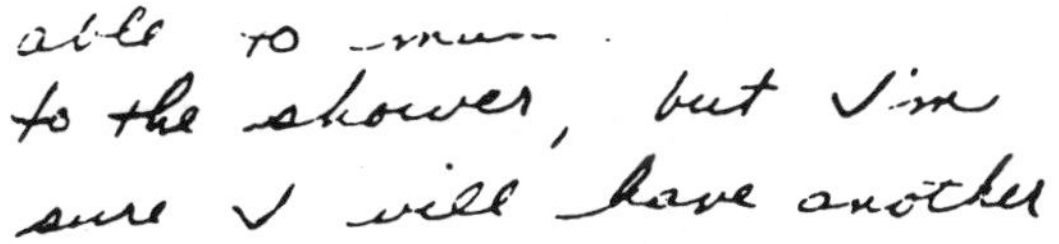

Fig. 46

Upward rising line direction reveals the writer's zeal. The reason for this pushing spirit may be elation—or anger—but whatever it is, your emotions are involved so much that you cannot stay on the straight and narrow path of the conventional middle-zone baseline. Optimism may be inferred, as well as excitability and restlessness. Your organizational ability under these circumstances may be either intensified or impaired, depending on other factors in the self-image.

Downward Line Direction

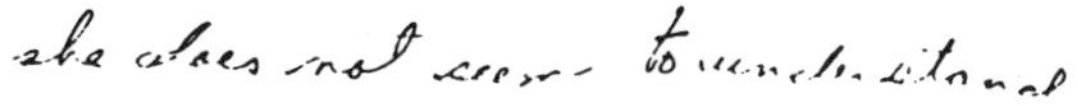

Fig. 47

Downward line direction often accompanies fatigue and depression. Pessimism may be the result of chronic or temporary tiredness. As the arm droops in writing, so does the accompanying graphic line, indicating slackness and lessened effort. Depressing the line downward habitually suggests lack of courage and push on the writer's part.

Evaluating a writing sample, the graphologist must take into consideration any neurological or physical

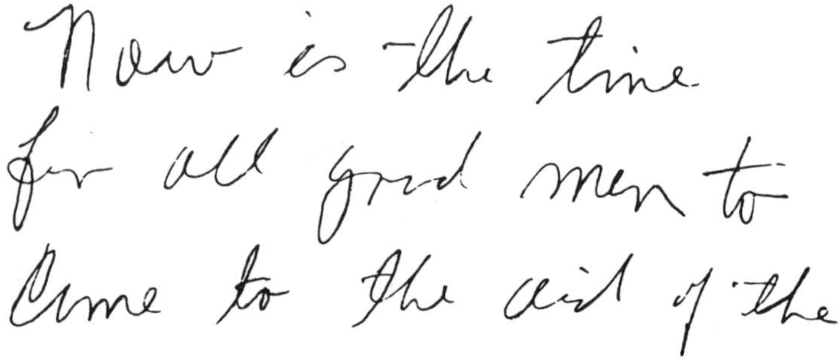

Fig. 48

impairment which can affect the organization of the handwriting. Graphodynamics are affected by the total being of the writer, as the writing in Figure 48 illustrates. The writer is nearly blind. His inconsistent slant, letter size, and uneven baseline are not negative features of his personality. He is an outgoing, dynamic person in spite of his disability. He is a musician who has made the most of his life.

Chapter 8

YOUR INTERESTS AND WRITING ZONES

One evening, at a large gathering, a sweet-faced, elderly lady approached the handwriting analyst. "I know you are interested in graphology," she said, "but I don't believe in it. I'm sure you can't guess from my handwriting what my talent is or what I'm especially interested in."

The analyst explained that an in-depth evaluation required at least a page of writing and accurate mathematical measurements besides. However, perhaps the personal pronoun and its relationship to the rest of the handwriting might serve as a clue to this lady's special talent. She wrote several sentences which included a few ppI's. The handwriting analyst noted that they were often connected to the word following. She noted also the strong emphasis placed upon the upper area of the writer's tall ego symbol shown in Figure 49.

"Your self-image has a great deal to do with going out to people," the analyst ventured. "You relate to them in a very easy manner and probably feel the need to express yourself fluently. But I also notice an apparent contrast; there must be a strong interest on your part in philosophy or ethical concepts. Your talent probably has something to do with the visionary, for you seem to emphasize

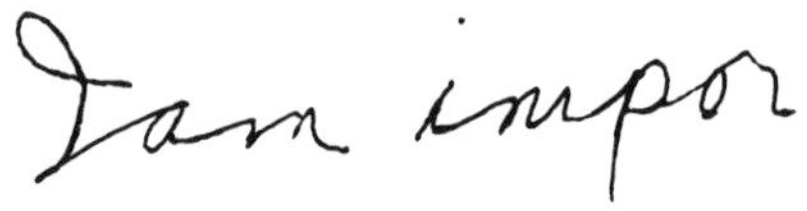

Fig. 49

out-of-this-world experiences. Yet, you do at the same time appear to bring your views down to other people's level."

The handwriting skeptic stared. "I don't believe it!" she exclaimed. "Do you know what I am? I'm a spiritualist."

A practicing medium, she felt that she used her special talent to help others. She relayed messages from the spirit world to those who needed comfort. She appeared to possess an unusual ability to communicate with both worlds—the "down here" and the "up there." She indicated that she possessed ESP. The emphasis on her personal pronoun showed interests which were definitely in the upper zone of writing.

Zonal relationships in handwriting were discovered by the Swiss psychologist, Dr. Max Pulver (1889-1952). He divided handwriting into three horizontal sections called zones.

Analogies are numerous concerning tri-zonal relationships. For example, in Christian theology there is a heaven above, a hell below and men on earth in the middle. Verbal expressions such as "rising in esteem", "high and mighty", "feet on the ground", "walking on air", "down in the dumps", suggest commonly accepted zonal relationships in everyday language.

Upper Zone
Middle Zone
Lower Zone

Fig. 50

Just as metaphysical thinkers have divided man into three parts: mind, body and soul, so the three giants of modern psychology also became involved many years ago in the "parts" of man. Simply put, Sigmund Freud dealt primarily with the libido, the sexual orientation of the psychological *drives* of the individual. This is represented in part by the lower zone of handwriting. Carl Jung dealt with the *collective unconscious* of mankind, the symbolic and spiritual aspects of our nature, represented by the upper zone of writing. Alfred Adler emphasized the cooperative *social interests* of the person, represented by the middle zone of writing.

- Upper zone loops are those which extend upward, such as f, h, k, l, and t. Emphasis on this writing area symbolizes orientation toward a more abstract plane of existence. It is on this level that man rises from his mundane interest in the here-and-now and

SYMBOLIC PROGRESSION OF THE
COPYBOOK *I*

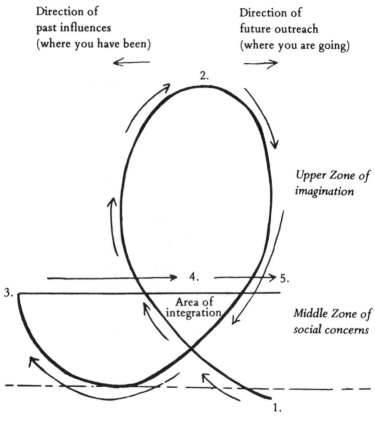

Direction of
past influences
(where you have been)

Direction of
future outreach
(where you are going)

2.

*Upper Zone of
imagination*

4. ⟶ 5.

Area of
integration

*Middle Zone of
social concerns*

3.

1.

*Lower Zone of
material and
physical needs*

Fig. 52

moves toward more philosophical considerations. Over extended letters may be a sign of aspiration or creativity, or perhaps of an unrealistic self-image.

- Middle zone letters are those with no extension, such as a, c, e, i, n, o, and s. Middle zone orientation of writing suggests interest in daily activities and the realm of practical reality. It is the center of handwriting, the area of conscious adaptation to routine. The middle zone is concerned with the forces of the social reality and interaction with others.

- The lower zone is where the lower extensions of letters such as g, j, p, q, and y fall. Lower zone emphasis symbolizes orientation to the material and physical aspects of life. It may also suggest sensual interests. Emphasis on the lower zone reflects the writer's primary motives of self-preservation and the satisfaction of his basic needs, including the sex drive.

The chart of the basic copybook *I* in Figure 51 illustrates the zonal divisions as well as the writing progressions of the *I*. Follow the progressive arrows (numbers 1 through 5) as you read the accompanying description of the symbolic significance of each area. Note how the writers of the following samples have made variations in the basic form. The emphasis each one has given to his personal pronoun says something about the writer's self-image.

- The starting point of the self-image is the springboard from which unconscious motives and physical and emotional drives propel the writer up from the lower zone's instinctual demands into the realm of practicality.

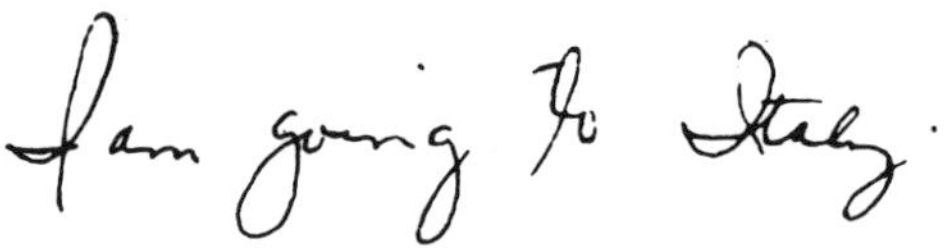

Fig. 52

Note the strong lower zone springboard stroke of the pp*I*. in Figure 52. The aggressive salesman who wrote this is highly motivated to succeed: he wants money and prestige. As a child, he never owned as much as a bicycle. His poverty-stricken family could not give him the things he wanted. Today his unconscious drives impel him into ambitious undertakings.

- Entering into the middle zone of every-day reality, the stroke moves beyond it and upward into the upper zone area of ideal aspirations, fantasies and philosophical considerations. This looped stroke encompasses both the regressive *past* and the progressive *future* impulses in its *leftward* and *rightward* movement.

The woman who wrote Figure 53 is an adherent of

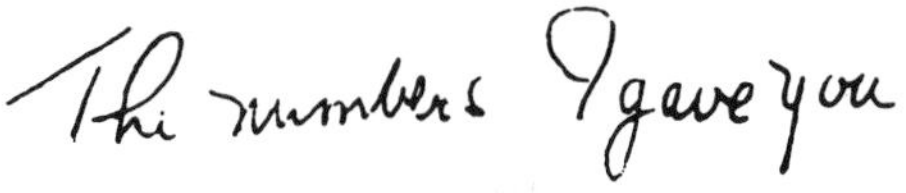

The numbers I gave you

Fig. 53

the Women's Liberation movement. She has many theories concerning the role of the superior woman. She was raised by her mother after her father deserted the family. Idealism and ethical principles appeal to this writer.

- Moving back down from the heights of imagination, the writer swings into the middle zone area of practical action again. Continuing to the left, the self encounters memories of past events which have been of influence.

I intend

Fig. 54

Figure 54 was written by a teenager. Her self-image is one of being where the action is and going around socially. Emphasis is in the area of the middle zone. She was raised by her father after her mother died when she was nine. Like many teenagers, her writing is large and rounded in the middle zone. Her writing is left-tending.

- Turning from the leftward motion to the right, the writer moves forward into an area of integration where past impressions merge with present influences.

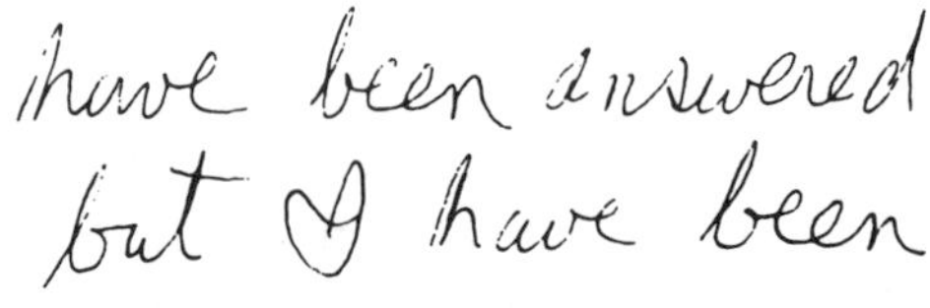

Fig. 55

Past memories hinder the self-image of the elderly gentleman who wrote Figure 55. He is an actor and author who now prefers solitude. He has suffered recurrent bouts of depression following manic activity. Both beginning and final *I* strokes are flaccid and incomplete. Nevertheless, good spacing and aesthetic considerations contribute to form level. He has emotional difficulty in integrating his experience of success with the present. He hesitates to move forward at this time.

- The final stroke moves outward toward the right, emphasizing the writer's outreach toward new accomplishments and future goals.

Fig. 56

The writer of Figure 56 is a seminary student who wishes to become a skilled counselor for his parishioners.

The strong, outflung ending of his *I* indicates that the writer moves out toward others. He has high hopes for the future and wishes to be of service to those around him.

Each of these five writers stresses certain symbolic areas in writing their pp*I*'s. The consistency of placement and/or writing emphasis within a zonal framework may indicate special interests. Beginning zonal placement of the *I* is on the baseline or slightly below. When this taught beginning area is changed (as in the case of the lady spiritualist) the personality may be an unusual one.

Middle Zone Emphasis

Evenness of placement of your *I* suggests your concern with reality and the working environment around you, to which you consciously adapt. Getting things done and moving along smoothly are classical aspects of the personality which consistently remains on the firm middle-zone baseline. Such writers are often the great do-ers of life who help others.

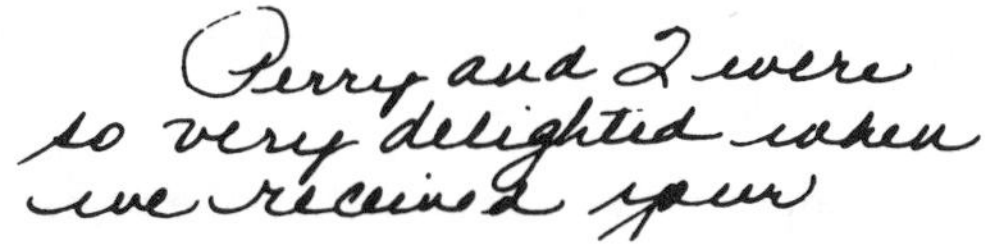

Fig. 57

The self-image of the young lady who wrote Figure 57 is one of practical accomplishment and social concern for others. Her handwriting is of high form level, and largely middle zone. Her *I* is placed squarely and firmly on the baseline. Emphasis in pattern and pressure is middle zone. She attends to business and knows what she wishes to accomplish. (She is newly married—note the importance she gives her husband's name compared to the size of her own pp*I*.)

Upper Zone Emphasis

The *I* which is "up in the air" or in some manner stresses the upper zone is not based upon middle-zone reality. Emphasis on this zone indicates a tendency on the writer's part to reach upward—beyond run-of-the-mill experiences. What this means with respect to the writer's personal acceptance of himself varies, of course. Implications may exist that he wishes to be different, or desires to place himself above ordinary matters. Or he may simply enjoy theoretical concepts.

Fig. 58

Outsize upper zone suggests that the writer of Figure 58 likes to deal with ideas and concepts. Practical considerations do not appeal to her and she is inclined to let her imagination run away with her. She visualizes herself as an unusual person beyond the ordinary.

Lower Zone Emphasis

The lower zone represents the forces of psychic and

physical energies. It may incorporate the writer's interest in material things, his past experiences and his instinctual drives. The area of the lower zone most often encompasses motives of the conscious life which may be unrecognized by the writer. Erotic urges and the personal instinct for pleasure and self-preservation are involved. It is concerned in part with the biological imperative which propels an organism to activity.

Involvement beyond the ordinary with the lower zone suggests the writer's concern with physical or material things, as well as the unconscious effect of past experiences. The "material" in this instance refers not merely to money or possessions, (although it may), but often to the writer's concern with whatever symbolizes love or power to him. How his concern with these elements in his life may manifest itself varies widely.

Perception through the physical senses is important to you, if you are a lower zone writer. For example, you may feel that you were or are deprived of love, money, or sex. This may be the case, or the opposite may have happened: you were richly indulged and never satisfied with less.

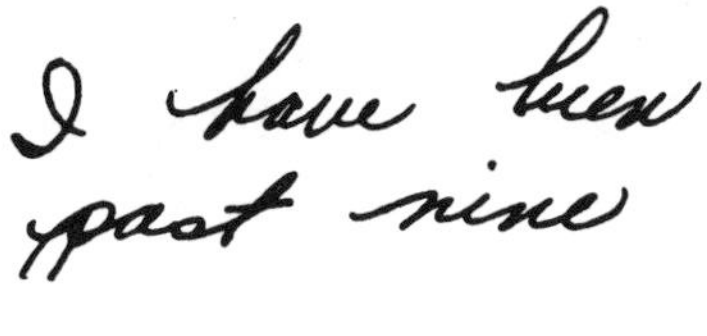

Fig. 59

Consistent lower-zone emphasis of the pp*I* as in

Figure 59 suggests some longstanding involvement with some of these factors. Energy may be important to you, perhaps because you have an excessive amount of drive, or because of too little. A down-flung *I* emphasizes preoccupation with past experiences tied in with your self-concept. Lower zone emphasis may also reveal an interest in the motives of others: seeking to understand others may become a source of security to the writer.

Fig. 60

The *I* which is often placed below the writing baseline suggests that the writer feels inadequate in relation to other people.

The self-image of the 28-year-old man who wrote Figure 60 is still hinging in great part upon his preoccupation with the past, conflicts with his mother and the loss of his father when he was a youngster. An outdoor buff, he is a physical culture enthusiast and a "regular" at "Muscle Beach" in California. He is preoccupied with his appearance as a virile male. Although the writer is interested in philosophical concepts, most writing pressure and pattern lies in the lower zone.

Chapter 9

TO LEAD OR TO NEED

A corollary exists between the pressures of leadership and graphological pressure as the writer bears down upon the paper. A person in the demanding role of leadership—be it in government, business, or the professions—is often referred to as being under great pressure. Or we hear such expressions as "high pressure job," "he couldn't take the pressure, so he quit," or a person is described as having "lots of push."

The writing in Figure 61 belongs to a young man who is the president of a successful chemical company. He is a self-confident leader, as his writing pressure and personal pronoun *I* suggest. The high form level of the writing as well as the strong writing pressure which embosses the underside of the paper reflect the dynamic aspects of the personality. The strong feelings of this writer are conveyed by his upward writing line (habitual) and flying t-bars. He is an enthusiastic, forward looking individual who likes people and enjoys living creatively. A strong and positive sense of self is witnessed by the tall, well-formed personal pronoun. Its rightward motion and sharpness are in

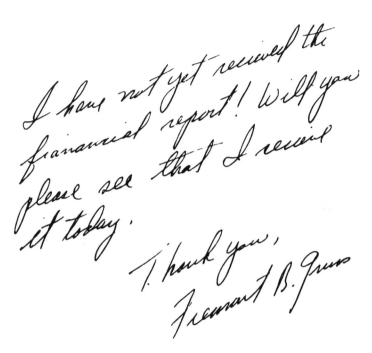

Fig. 61

harmony with the entire writing. The high form level reflects the writer's integrated personality.

Leadership potential depends a great deal upon how deeply and strongly you feel about things. In other words, your particular emotional memory of events, persons and places plays an important part in how much physical and psychic energy you are willing and able to invest in a particular pursuit. Leadership seems to accrue to those individuals who care enough consistently to do their very best.

Just as a loud voice or excessive gesturing indicates a person's desire to emphasize a point and underline a message, so a heavy pressure in handwriting implies extra emphasis and extra energy. In behavioral studies, it is found that the amount of energy taken to perform a task is reduced with the person's ability to master it: as he increases his motor skill, the individual uses less energy to accomplish a task.

Almost everybody has observed a child as he is learning to write. His entire body takes part in the performance: he bobs his head, cranes his neck and even twists his tongue. His entire torso appears involved with effort. He may twine his legs around the chair and jiggle his feet. In his beginning efforts he emphasizes total bodily effort and movement in what he is learning to master. The entire body participating in what will ultimately seem a simple manual performance is expressive of the individual's manner of assimilation. There is, first, general effort and finally a synergized, specific movement which results in smooth mastery.

Similar concentration is required for learning a "job." However, when proficiency has been achieved and *still* the same early high-level energy is channeled into the work, one can deduce that the individual feels some tension or emotional recall which causes him to continue putting forth extra effort. In spite of success, he keeps on trying as hard as if he were not yet successful.

This kind of drive appears to be the force behind many successful men who work night and day to accomplish their goals and keep right on working. Habit plays a part and creative desire impells. The memory of past success or failure cannot be under-estimated as a spur and propelling trait in personal achievement.

These same traits apply to handwriting: deep feelings plus energy go hand-in-hand with writing pressure which goes deep into the paper. The more strongly a writer feels about what he is writing, the more strongly he is apt to push pen into paper. Such "push" is equated with both physical energy and emotional recall.

Heavy pressured writing, in most cases, can be felt through the back of the paper with the fingertips. In its most positive aspects, this feelable pressure suggests will-power and enthusiasm. The writer remembers and reinforces his emotional recall of past events. The ability to maintain heavy writing pressure fades with age in many instances: it takes energy and denotes effort on the writer's part to keep up the pace.

It is not surprising that graphological firms dealing with personnel consider writing pressure important. For to write quickly and easily, as well as deeply, is often symbolic of depth of energy and emotion, consistency of action and self-actualization. Potential for leadership of some kind may be expressed this way.

However, there is another side of the coin to this emotional go-power. An unusually retentive memory may give the owner no rest as he dwells upon past events. Such brooding is a handicap: he forfeits a more easy-going attitude which would keep him in better emotional balance.

For example, the handwriting in Figure 62 is that of a nice-appearing young man whose combination of great

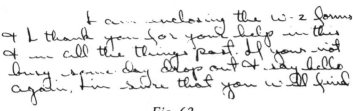

Fig. 62

physical energy and persistent emotional memory might well place him high on a list for potential leaders. He has a quick and clever mind and has travelled all over the world. A foundling, he never knew his parents and was placed in a series of foster homes. A group of bad experiences turned him against society, and particularly against women. He could not forgive or forget the woman who had first deserted him: his mother. Excessive tension caused him almost to bleed to death from ulcers on two occasions before he was nineteen. A history of petty crimes climaxed in a rape-slaying for which he is now serving a life sentence. This potentially capable man was unable to channel productively whatever leadership abilities he possessed. Note the deep, incised pressure and squeezed personal pronoun. The dug-in muddiness and meagerness of the *I*, plus tremor, spell trouble in the self-concept.

Although we associate heavy pressure with energy and leadership, lightness of pressure is not necessarily negative. Well-articulated yet quickly executed writing suggests resiliency and the ability to adapt to new situations. Long-term emotional involvement may not be the writer's forte, however. If you write with light pressure and nevertheless find yourself eventually a chairman or president, the chances are that your flexibility and "bounce-back" accomplish things which would exhaust a harder driving individual. Lightly written script may also suggest an impersonal, objective attitude. The writer may view himself as an observer rather than as a participant in events. He may not take himself or things with undue seriousness.

Moderately pressured handwriting is that which can just barely be felt on the reverse side of ordinary bond paper. This suggests a give-and-take in social relations dealing with emotional recall. Changes in writing pressure suggest ambivalence or discomfort concerning the self, particularly when the pp*I* is involved.

The writers of Figures 63 and 64 have two things in common: each wrote his personal pronoun with much less weight than the rest of his script. Spotty pressure is also evident in both handwritings. Why should the pen barely touch paper when the ego symbol is written?

Fig. 63

The writer of Figure 63 was 22 years old and in the Navy when he wrote these words: his *I* is barely visible.

Fig. 64

The writer of Figure 64 was 44 years old when he penned his weak-looking *I* and small signature with its downhill slant. At that time he was an importer and a salesman in a foreign country. He had suffered a nervous collapse several years before but appeared to have recovered sufficiently to go back to his work.

Both of these men, judging from outward appearance, had a great deal to live for. But both took their own life shortly after writing these words. The superficial, light pressure which characterizes each of these ego symbols exemplifies lack of energy and commitment toward the self.

Sometimes human potential remains inactive and unrealized because other essential needs predominate or other yearnings remain unsatisfied. Human growth depends upon basic fulfillments: Each of us wants to feel appreciated, wanted and needed. Genuine love, warmth and respect are aspects of living that keep us going day after day. If these essentials of life are denied us, we feel anxious and uncertain over the quality of our self-image. We cannot know clearly what we really are if we feel rejected and the target of hostility. We become unable to organize our inner forces to restore good order within ourselves or to channel our energies and commitments into positive goals.

Psychologists have long recognized that faulty attitudes about oneself may find expression in poor behavior patterns. The ego symbol spotlights unfulfilled needs that stifle latent abilities. Here are a few examples:

The Need for Courage
The writer of Figure 65 is a National Merit Scholar,

This summer I plan to

Fig. 65

aged 17, who is both able and conscientious. However, he is not confident about his abilities and is self-centered. (Note the small size and tightly looped formation of the pp*I*.) Conflicting needs for self-protection keep him from taking the risk of leadership.

The Need for Protection

The young lady, aged 20, who wrote Figure 66 is all wrapped up in herself. She has been pampered by her parents and likes being babied. The foetal-like shape of her

I Believe a small

Fig. 66

I and flaccid structure of its rounded form testify to her need for a buffer against the world.

The Need for Affection

I believe that

Fig. 67

Marcia, age 16, who penned Figure 67, is a charming young girl whose innocent brown eyes do not convey the depth of her need for love. She has tried to win the affection and attention of her parents away from a favored younger brother throughout the years. Lately she has been arrested for shop-lifting things she can well afford to buy. She likes possessions (note the beginning acquisitive hook and long terminal hook.) She feels more loved when she owns things she doesn't need.

The Need for Attention

Fig. 68

Excessive height and width of the *I* in Figure 68 shows the interest of this young writer, age 23, in asserting herself. Her outgoing personality is an asset to her in her job as a receptionist in a theatrical agency.

The Need for Communication

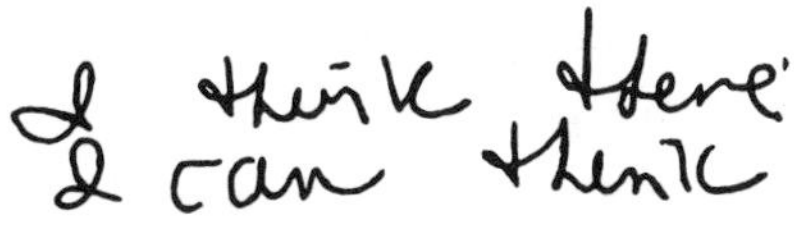

Fig. 69

The writer of Figure 69, age 25, is unsure of herself, as the small size of the *I* in relation to the middle zone height shows. She would like to have more friends: she goes out to others—the second ego symbol is more closely spaced than the first—but is inconsistent. Her sociability, however, is not so much genuine interest in others as self-concern, shown by the vertical slant.

The Need for Romance

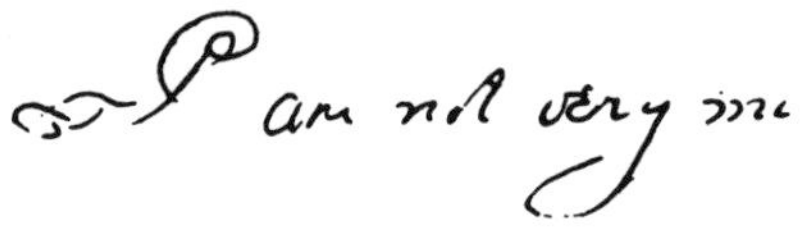

Fig. 70

This ornately decorated *I* in Figure 70 tells us that the writer, age 25, seeks to reassure himself. He calls attention to himself in ways that are out of the ordinary: he likes to impress and is in turn impressed with the unusual or romantic. As his middle and lower zone elaborations suggest, he surrounds himself with baroque, exotic accessories and dresses in a colorful fashion. Upper zone emphasis indicates that he dreams of far-out adventure. The writing pressure is light: this writer is an escapist rather than a plain dealer.

The Need for Leadership

Fig. 71

The writer of Figure 71 is a football star, age 20,

popular and aggressive. Note the extreme height of the ego symbol, showing vanity and need to dominate. The narrow width offers a clue as to his inner self-consciousness: he requires being in command in order to feel worthwhile. He has little insight into his motives of leadership, as the restricted loop signifies.

Chapter 10

THE COMPENSATING YOU

Each of us has areas of real or fancied weakness: we may be (or think we are) too tall or too short, too thin or too fat, not as bright as we might be, disfigured, poor or unattractive. With or without justification, we feel insecure, and to defend our ego against this insecurity, we may put extra effort and discipline into substituting some acceptable trait for our real or imagined deficiency. As a consequence, we may actually excell—or exceed in accomplishments—those individuals whose egos are not thus threatened.

This process of defending the ego is termed *compensation*—or, when carried to extremes, over-compensation. Society benefits when a man expends his energy to eliminate causes of poverty because his own impoverished childhood is still vivid in his mind. And most of us are familiar with the statement that the history of the world would have been different had Napoleon been one foot taller than he was.

Efforts to avoid inner disorganization, to ease anxiety, will be sought through compensatory behavior.

We often draw mistaken conclusions regarding the meaning of what happens to us; when our ego is threatened, we must make amends for some lack or loss of status because we wish to lessen or to forget some deficiency which we think we have. These reactions to fear or anxiety are indicated at times within the pp*I*.

Do You "Reverse" Your *I*?

What does it suggest if, in the writing of the pp*I*, you reverse your progression: that is, you "begin" at the "end" and "end" at the "beginning" of the copybook model?

Taught I

Most people who "reverse" the copybook model are not aware of doing it, and some left-handed writers may have found it more comfortable to write in this fashion. Or, the teacher may not have taught the Palmer or Zaner-Bloser method properly.

Reversed I Under normal conditions, however, the *I* begins toward the left and ends at the right.

Determining the actual process of forming the *I* is difficult for the untrained eye. It will be revealed through writing *pressure*. Although the copybook form may appear to be conventionally written, the pressure will be reversed. What should be a down stroke, will be an upstroke with light pressure; what should be an upstroke with light pressure will actually be a heavier pressured downstroke.

When you reverse your *I* you are expressing yourself in a distinctive manner which is not easily detected or understood. By establishing a unique method of writing the ego symbol, you are unconsciously affirming your sense of worth, you are decidedly doing your own thing. A backward=written *I* meets a private need for originality much as a special style of clothing or hair style does. Creativity of the writer may be affirmed further if the rest of the writing is full of simplified short-cuts and of high form level.

Covert defiance is apt to be indicated by this manner of self-expression. Reversal is not ordinary. It could be that at the time of learning to write, the teacher was disliked or some situation brought out a negative reaction on the writer's part. Whatever the reason, it appears that the writer is *privately having his own way*. Ability to assess himself and manage to maintain his own manner of doing things may be compensatory devices of the reverse *I* writer. How much of an asset or liability this may be to him depends upon the manner in which these characteristics are used.

In the following pages are some samples of handwritings containing reversed *I*'s written like the small letter l.

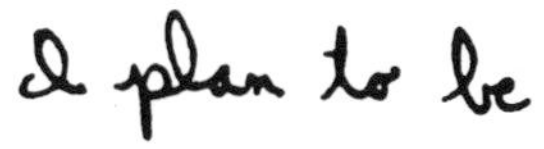

Fig. 72

The writer of Figure 72, age 18, quietly goes her own way in spite of her alcoholic father and hopes to become a social worker. She is shy but determined in her plans.

Fig. 73

His family considers children as simply trouble, and the young man, age 20, who wrote Figure 73 has a distorted view of himself. He has had problems in school and resents authority. (Note that the capital *I* in the word *If* is not reversed.)

Fig. 74

The writer of Figure 74, age 19, has been on drugs for a year. Prior to that time, she was a good student. The separation of her parents was a blow to her. She doesn't trust men and says she needs a father.

Fig. 75

The writer of Figure 75, age 27, starts her pp*I* with a long backswing which circles forward and goes counter-clockwise. She came from a harmonious home and was doted on by her father.

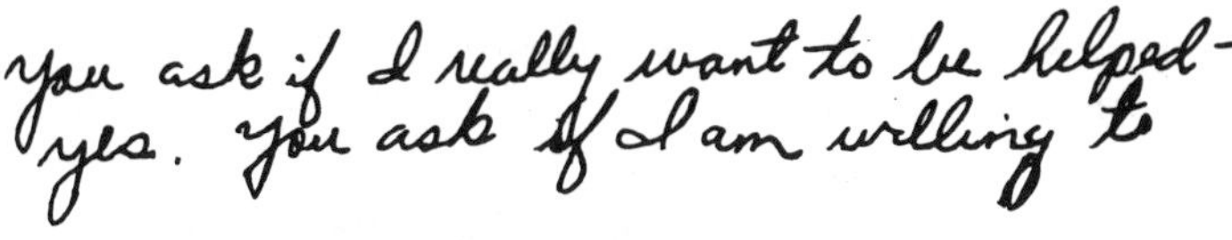

*you ask if I really want to be helped—
yes. you ask if I am willing to*

Fig. 76

The reversed *I* in Figure 76 speaks of the writer's defiance. He is in constant trouble with the law. Although he has a charming personality and appears contrite, he is inclined to manipulate those around him. He never stays long out of trouble.

Do You Displace Your Pressure?

What does it indicate if the pressure of your writing stroke is just the opposite of normal: the upstroke heavy—instead of light—and/or the downstroke light—instead of heavy?

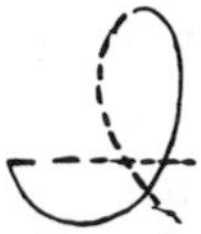

Normal

If you write your ego symbol in this manner, even though you begin and end properly, the chances are that the rest of your writing will reveal displacement in the up and down strokes, particularly on the lower zone loops such as f, g, j, p, y. Displaced pressure is evident in Figure 77: note the heaviness of the upstroke on the lower zone *g* and the heavy horizontal pressure on the pp*I*.

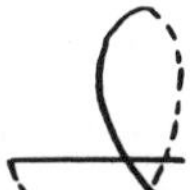

Displaced

Displaced pressure reveals stress on the part of the writer. (The reversed *I* is not necessarily one with displaced pressure, however. If it were both reversed and had displaced pressure, it would appear "normal" as in Figure 77.)

Fig. 77

When much of the writing contains displaced pressure, chances are that the writer feels a need to overcome frustration. Often this reversal may prove only temporary; once the crisis is over, the writing reverts to the norm. When there is doubt concerning the manner in which the pp*I* is actually written, it is necessary for the analyst to watch the letters being formed.

To displace pressure within the pp*I* actually demands a great deal of muscular control and self-discipline. When the pressure is also split in the text, the actualization of these strenuous demands suggests blocking from consciousness of some frightening or hurtful memories. Such displacement of efforts—symbolized by the pressure—is consistent with the writer's extreme need to control his environment. Such efforts, however, put a lid upon the free expression and psychic energies of the writer.

Whether temporary or permanent, displacement of pressure indicates displacement of energies; the writer is apt to compensate in some manner to keep his emotional balance. Sublimation of his energies may prove productive if the writer channels them successfully into his work.

Commitment to activity is often expressed by displacement of writing pressure. Such writers may be enthusiastic, able and be potent forces in our society. Horizontal strokes such as t-bars may be unusually long and heavy, and the writer may possess the habit of underlining his written words for emphasis.

Fig. 78

On the negative side, frustration may prove a great burden, too much for the writer of Figure 78. He has had a history of molesting little girls, although he is a choir director and a capable businessman.

Does Your *I* Have Unusual Design?

What does it indicate if your pp*I* is shaped like a heart? Or a number? Or a music or art symbol? Another letter?

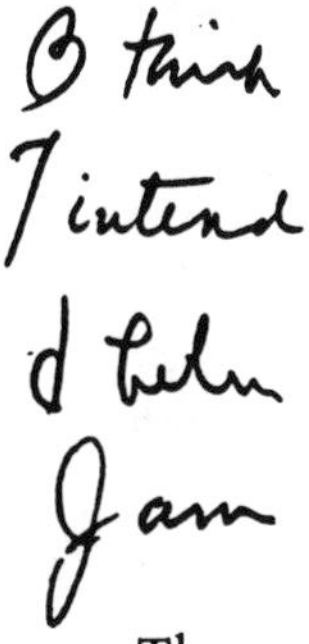

If you wish to identify with people, careers or talents which you admire, perhaps your ego symbol will express this wish. A pp*I* in the shape of an initial (your own or somebody else's) may offer a clue as to where your deepest interests lie. A sword, a whip or a club-like *I* may express your dissatisfaction.

The writer of Figure 79 uses the same formation in his signature and personal pronoun.

Fig. 79

The seminary student who wrote Figure 80 was raised by parents who gave him many material things, but not as much of their intimacy or time as he wanted. Instead of a hug, he was apt to get a $10 bill. He felt "bought off" with money. Note the dollar sign in the writer's pp*I*.

Fig. 80

Caring intensely about the self and being frustrated is sometimes indicated in *I* symbols which are involved in loops and angles. Self-conscious lack of positive identification is suggested by elaboration of the ego symbol.

If you seek compensatory relief from anxiety concerning your self-worth by using drugs or alcohol excessively, the writing may show distorted forms, blotched thickness, spotty diggings into the paper and a shivering quality to the ductus (writing stroke) which are apparent to the analyst.

Figure 81 is written by a 38-year-old hard-core heroin addict who spent a good portion of his life in jails. The psychologist's report, in part, states:

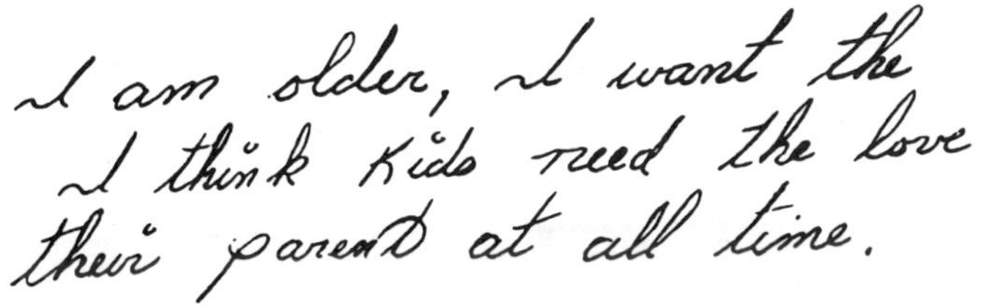

*I am older, I want the
I think kids need the love
their parents at all time.*

Fig. 81

There is no doubt that this man spends a great deal of time setting up some favorable image of himself to project to others. He is idealistic, keeps others at a distance, and is not motivated to seek a better understanding of himself. His activities are directed towards fighting off an awareness of homosexual inclinations, and finding someone to take care of him. He is married to another hard-core addict. For him, escape in drugs is an ideal way to avoid being an adult. When he is high, he talks in philosophical overtones and avoids discussing the plain facts of reality.

The two ego symbols of the killer Zodiac were mentioned on page 36. One *I* was in tiny lower case, the other overblown, as shown in Figure 82.

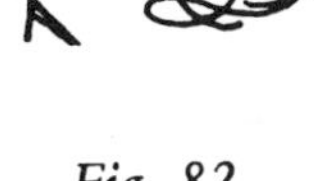

Fig. 82

Feeling powerless, Zodiac compensated by seeking notoriety through murder. Feelings of self-pity and helplessness are apt to be overcompensated for by individuals who cannot see themselves as productive, capable members of society.

Chapter 11

COPING WITH ANXIETY

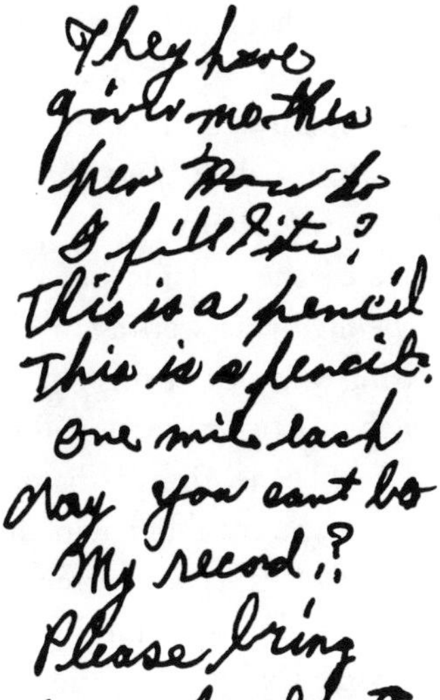

Fig. 83

The middle-aged gentleman who wrote Figure 83 has been diagnosed as paranoid. He is a deeply troubled person; his handwriting, too, is troubled. Note its narrowness,

113

angularity, and stiff appearance. There is a shivering quality to the ductus, letters grow vertically with subsequent neglect of the horizontal connections. There is a generalized confusion in the uneven pressure and entire spatial organization. All this applies to the written ego symbol as well; its misshapen form suggests that the writer's self-concept is disturbed.

Life is an adaptive effort. Some of us achieve, and maintain, enough equilibrium to function in a manner which seems normal. Others fail: their emotional conflicts have been severe enough to incapacitate them. We all suffer from fears caused by circumstances, or from anxiety from within. Sometimes fear and anxiety are Siamese twins—we cannot separate them.

Faulty notions of the self may at times be expressed in faulty *writing behavior* as well as in maladaptive *social behavior*. The writing samples in this chapter were all done by persons who have not functioned well in society.

Just as there can be no simple diagnosis of cause and effect with respect to the total behavior pattern, there can be no simple diagnosis of cause and effect with respect to a person's writing. It is the opinion of this graphologist, however, that if a writer's pp*I* is particularly noteworthy, there is usually a reason.

The *I* In Trouble

- *The Tremulous I:* The inability to hold the pen steady is one of the first signs of tension. You may shake when something upsets you emotionally or physically. When tremor in handwriting is not due to neurological or physiological factors (age, fatigue, illness, drugs or alcohol) one may look to the inner self.

• *The Hesitant I:* Sudden, unpremeditated stops are sometimes not noticeable except through a magnifying glass. Whether or not they are easy to see, they slow down or may totally disrupt the movement over the paper. Such little stops are sometimes caused by hesitation or inhibition. Spottiness in writing is associated with lack of whole-hearted commitment.

• *The Mended I:* Retouching or mending of writing suggests tendencies toward uneasiness and nervousness. Whether such covering-up is done habitually or only now and then, it reveals a desire to change things. You may feel vaguely threatened as you mend your ego symbol.

• *The Retraced I:* Retracing bolsters the writing: there appears to be some desire for camouflage or support. Retracing also carries implications of repression: unconscious blocking out of unacceptable or painful memories. (In passing, it may be noted that even young children may be sensitive to the "hiding" effects of overlay: it has been demonstrated at various times that youngsters who chose to place colors over one another in their paintings tended to be more "repressed" than those using separate color placement.)

- *The Slow I:* Slow writing is not as rhythmical as fast writing. Just as ragged rhythm suggests impaired vitality, so slow script is symptomatic of a checking of spontaneous impulses. Creative persons who are not fearful of results may have writing which to the untrained eye appears grossly irregular, but which actually possesses positive natural qualities. Slow writing, on the other hand, may appear nicely regular but still lack qualities of freedom.

- *The Uneven I:* Unevenness in writing is associated with sensitiveness. The *I* which is uneven in such factors as size, speed, pressure, slant, hints at excitability. Negatively, it may echo the undisciplined personality, especially if these factors add up to low form level.

- *The Fragmented I:* Broken strokes are symptoms of hampered movement, expressive of the individual who finds difficulty in integrating various parts into a consistent whole. Logical assessment of his self-image may be impaired.

The Excessive I:
- *Over-controlled* writing suggests deep feelings which the writer is afraid to admit. In such

instances, he may be rather slavish about sticking to the copybook or utilize props such as rulers or lined paper to make his writing more precise or pretty. Likewise, writing which is backhand or vertical, but very deeply incised into the paper, implies strong emotions which the writer seeks to suppress. Squeezed-together writing likewise carries these implications.

- *Over-elaborated* script may be symptomatic of the writer's need for ego enhancement. Decorative, embellishing loops and circles suggest a facade which conceals the "real" individual. Hooks (large or small catches at beginning or ending strokes) connote a need for grasping and holding on to things or ideas which symbolize security to the writer.

- *Uncommonly angular, garland, arcade* or *thread* writings hint at personality factors which emphasize negative aspects of their symbolic meanings. For example, the humped or circular *I* points to a self-image in need of protection. (There are actual instances where the personal pronoun is written with a separate circle placed around it.) Excessive thread suggests a running away from scrutiny; garlands are often associated with passiveness, angles with anger.

- *Puffed-up* or *deflated size* reflect the writer's preoccupation with the self. Excessive size connotes a need for self-assertion; "baby" size hints at self-negation.

- *Overly-slanted* writing indicates intensely personal response. Reclined ego symbols suggest vulnerability to the environment, tendencies to hysteria, or openness to trivial concerns. Far-to-the-left ego symbols, on the other hand, imply a shunning of forward movement and aversion to social contact.

- *Extremes of pressure and/or non-pressure* exemplify extremes of psychic energy. Heaviness is symbolic of resistance met and overcome: positive value is lost when imprinting impedes—actually as well as symbolically—the writing movement. Lightness is caused by a skimming over the writing surface: loss of initiative, lethargy or shallow thinking may be symptoms of chronic inner anxiety.

Compensation for real or imagined inadequacies may lead to striking accomplishments. On the other hand, when overcompensation fails, pathological processes may be set in motion and neurotic, or even psychotic, symptoms may appear. The discouraged person may withdraw from the demands of life to seek greater security in a "private" world—a release from the struggle—as did the writers of Figures 84 and 85.

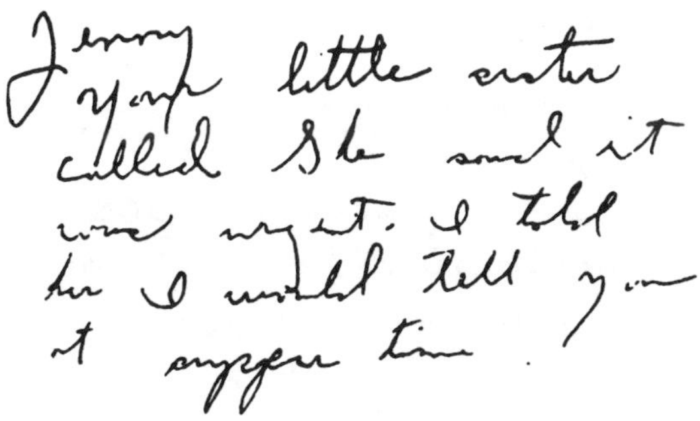

Fig. 84

The writer of Figure 84 is a middle-aged woman. She is presently staying in a Halfway House trying to adjust to society after a period in a mental institution. She has been extremely dependent upon her parents and finds it difficult to make decisions. Note the reclined and reversed *I*, with its uneven and spotty appearance. Angularity and disharmonious letter connections contribute to the appearance of slow writing, in spite of the more rapid thread tendencies. A conflict between standing still and going ahead exists. The smallness of the ego symbol indicates the frail self-image of this writer. The pressed-down writing of the middle zone suggests a depression which is probably chronic.

The little girl who wrote Figure 85 hanged herself when whe was twelve, a year after writing this. She had been in a series of foster homes most of her life, after

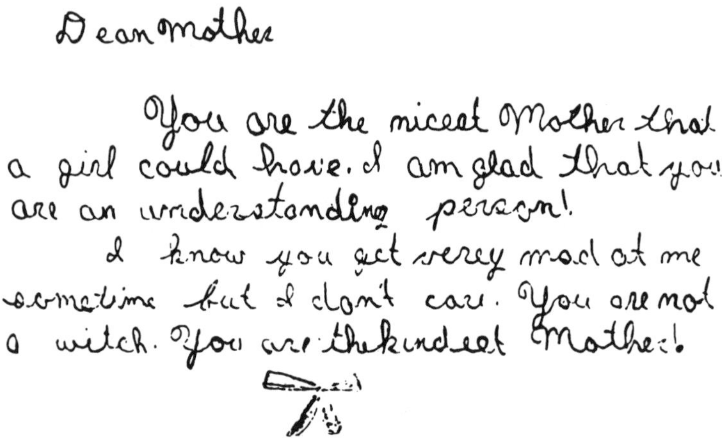
Dear Mother

You are the nicest Mother that a girl could have. I am glad that you are an understanding person!

I know you get verey mad at me sometime but I don't care. You are not a witch. You are the kindest Mother!

Fig. 85

being removed from an abusive and disturbed mother. The foster mother to whom this letter is addressed says that Frances wanted love, but was unable to accept it. There are at present no specific norms or constructs for children's writing, yet the graphologist may surmise that Frances had ego conflicts and felt alienated at the time of this writing: note the erratic spacing and displaced pressure of the ego symbols, which are isolated and small; her signature, too, is shrunken.

No material on graphology can be complete without a discussion of rhythm, which is an integral part of harmony within the organism. Balance is maintained by unconscious perception of wideness versus narrowness, largeness versus smallness, etc. The normal handwriting balances itself between these extremes, with a continuum of contraction and release between brain and hand, nerve and muscle. Physiologically, neurologically, and psychologically, the structure must be unified for optimum performance.

The downstroke is the more consciously controlled stroke. The writer regulates its size, length and shape, as well as its speed and pressure. Individual letters may be identified by the downstroke—erasure of written downstrokes cause the letter forms to be lost. Upstrokes, however, may be eliminated and the letter is usually still recognizable.

Disturbance of the light-heavy beat of up and down strokes alters writing appearance as well as rhythm. Loss of the release quality of the upstroke is indicative of a loss of interior psychic release by the ego.

Rhythm is equated psychologically with inward self-control and inner balance. It is outwardly symbolic of relatively constant relationships within the framework of the environment. In handwriting, of course, the "environment" is represented by the paper on which the writing path is traced; good organization of space is an integral part of good rhythm.

Spontaneity in handwriting is a part of rhythm. It is the opposite of rigidity or fixation of stroke. Such naturalness gives hint of impulses proceeding from natural personal impulses. Spontaneity is likewise opposed to conformity to exact pattern. For example, Chancery or Italic cursive script is still being taught and used. This highly stylized manner of writing owes its existence over the centuries to persons who enjoy form and tradition.

Yet, tremendous individual differences exist, and are encouraged, within the traditional letters: after rigorous and mechanical practicing of each structure, the writer is free to express his own uniqueness. This is the "art" at its peak.

Natural spontaneity of the written personal pronoun says something of the psychic courage of the writer, especially if the written form encompasses originality. When spontaneity is low, rhythm is disturbed and creative powers lessened. Convincing rhythm with total regularity of beat, in the positive sense, evidences sustained power to cope in an orderly fashion with impulsiveness.

Rhythm is not necessarily equated with evenness or repetition. Careful monotony is arhythmic rather than dynamically balanced. Recurring similar patterns must be developed with a harmonious interplay of various forms for high form level evaluation.

Since rhythm is related to good organization, arrangement and proportion must be considered in all aspects. Appropriate word and letter spacing, zonal balance, slant, direction of line, margins and over-all relation to background are part of total rhythmic integration. The pp*I* which is associated with the positive side of these elements may be classified as rhythmical and flexibily integrated.

While the previous and subsequent handwriting samples in this chapter lack positive harmony, it must be stressed that disunity and lack of "rhythm" occur in all strata of society. Both "successful" and "unsuccessful" persons may have damaging personality conflicts, and still have writing within the norm.

Wherever it exists, inner distress must find release. A person may overcompensate for exaggerated inferiority feelings by exaggerated aggression, or perhaps by withdrawing into depression or suicide.

Difficulties in learning and difficulties in social interest may be said to arise in part because of a faulty or inferior vision of the self. The victims of society and those who victimize society are alike—both are people who have assimilated a limited, or a stereotyped picture of their potentials. Such personalities become blocked because they have been built upon a biased definition of the self. For this reason, there is a fragile limit to psychological development and personal encounters with other people.

It has been said that prison offers the ultimate security for those unfortunates who need to experience constant mothering and reassurance. "Repeaters" may look to prison bars for escape from the competition and uncertainties of freedom. The womb-like prison cell may offer a haven.

The following samples were all written by male inmates of a large midwestern prison. The graphological character of each sample clearly suggests psychological damage to the self-image. The age, grade level, intelligence quotient and the crime committed are given with each sample. Note that in all cases the schooling was interrupted in spite of the inmate's adequate I.Q. The evaluation of both the graphologist and the psychologist are given in part with each sample.

The writer of Figure 86 is a 44-year-old man who is

incarcerated for murder. His grade level is 7.6, I.Q. 99.

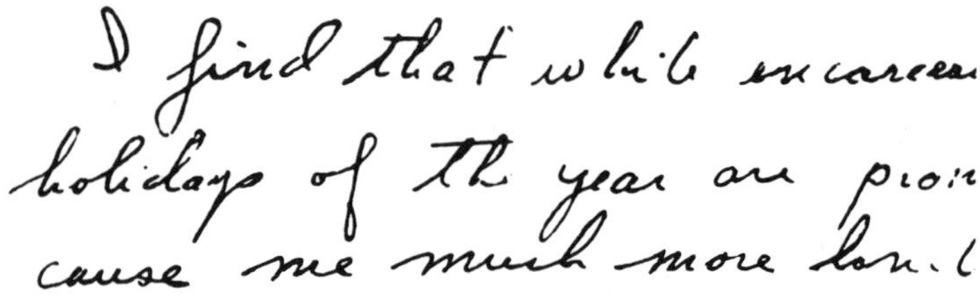

Fig. 86

From the graphologist's report: The writer's ego symbol moves to the left, away from general activity. He is a cause unto himself, as this factor and the tallness and careful precision of his pp*I* indicate. Nevertheless, displaced pressure suggests undue tension and hidden excitability. Fluidity of line suggests fluent thought and ability to communicate when it suits him to do so.

From the psychologist's report: A very calm and reserved person . . . a professional criminal for several years with narcotic involvement. He enters the psychological interview in a matter-of-fact and business-like manner. His figure-drawings and general demeanor tend to indicate that he is brighter than his scores would indicate.

The man who wrote Figure 87 is 43 years old. He was incarcerated for possession of drugs. His grade level is 8.6, I.Q. 102.

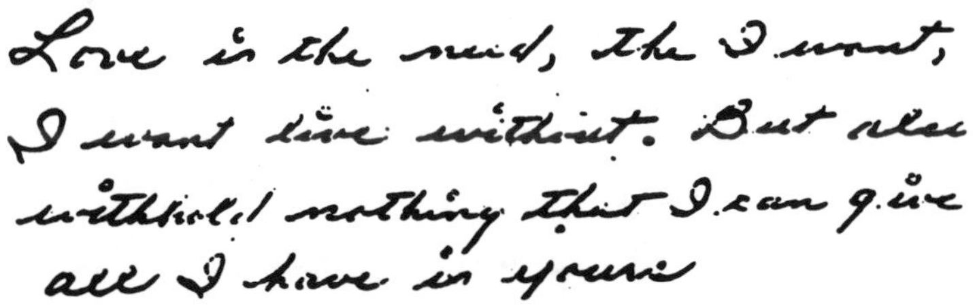

Fig. 87

From the graphologist's report: The writer is a yielding person, overly susceptible to his past and uncertain as to his actual identity. His open, reclined, differentiated pp*I*'s suggest that he has a hard time resisting temptation. Love of attention is indicated by the fancy *i*-dots; pastose line suggests a need for physical gratification. He has refined inclinations.

From the psychologist's report: Lacks social interest and social skills. Limited insight . . . lacks conventional goals and appears to be overly concerned about immediate personal satisfaction.

The writer of Figure 88 was incarcerated for rape. He is 28 years old. His grade level is 9.6, I.Q. 114.

From the graphologist's report: Defensiveness against the future, lack of insight and empathy are shown by the back-slanted *I* and narrowness of form. Excessive pressure shows strong emotionality with impulsive proclivities to act out his tensions. Lack of realistic goals and poor understanding of his potential handicap this individual.

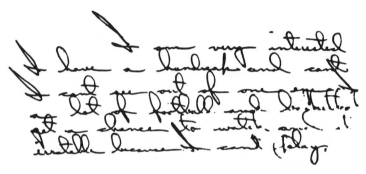

Fig. 88

From the psychologist's report: Personality data indicates a high degree of rigidity and very narrow interest range ... strong dependency needs and masculine self-concept concerns. Limited empathy in his personal relationships ... difficulty in dealing non-defensively with feelings.

The young man who wrote Figure 89 was sent to prison for rape. He is 27 years old. His grade level is 10.0, I.Q. 127.

From the graphologist's report: Muddiness suggests strong sensual needs. The writer is possessive and tenacious in what he does. Constricted writing and fluctuating slant and pressure show defensiveness and suppression of emotion. The pp*I*'s angularity, uneven pressure, left-tending up-in-the-air placement suggest an unrealistic self-image.

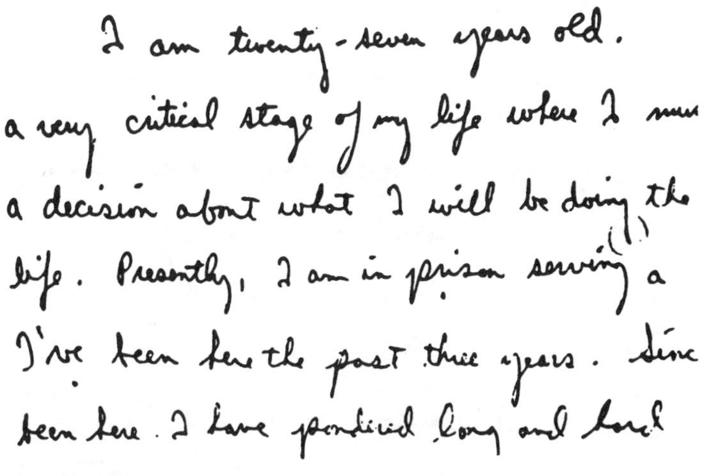

Fig. 89

From the psychologist's report: Anxiety-provoking topics cause him to retreat to vagueness and passive expressions of hostility ... attempts to control feelings ... little flexibility ... personality picture that is obsessive ... deflects feelings into intellectual channels ... much use of defense mechanism of reaction formation. Severe neurotic conflict.

The writer of Figure 90 is 31 years old. He was incarcerated for possession and sale of drugs. His grade level is 8.5, I.Q. 103.

From the graphologist's report: Tiny, yielding,

lower-case *i* as a personal pronoun suggest severe feelings of inadequacy and withdrawal. Excessive pastosity and muddiness of line shows inclination to enjoy or need sensuous, physically pleasureable sensations which excessive stimulation (drugs?) can produce. Needs escape.

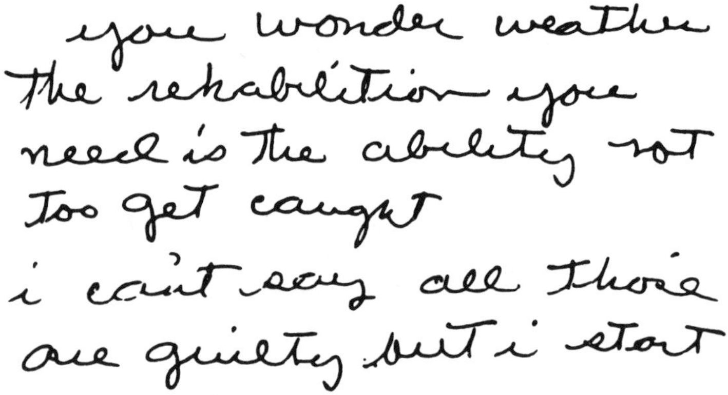

Fig. 90

From the psychologist's report: MMPI findings indicate emotional immaturity and dyssocial behavior . . . a basic inferiority complex . . . sexual confusion . . . deflated opinion of himself and his qualities; that is, confusion arising from a preoccupation with feelings of . . . impotence.

The man who wrote Figure 91 was sent to prison for felonious assault. He is 30 years old. His grade level is 8.3, I.Q. 101.

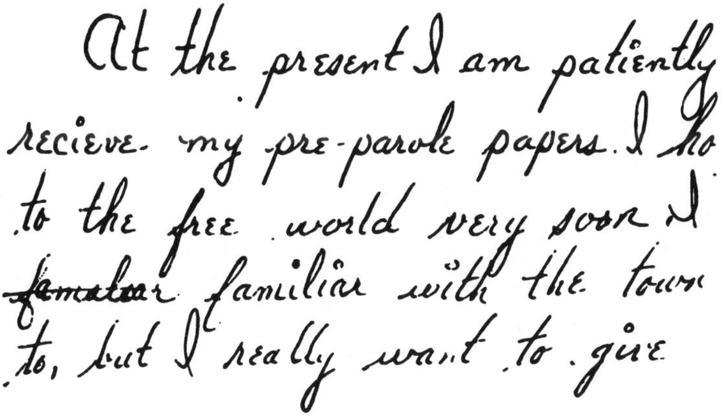

At the present I am patiently recieve my pre-parole papers. I ho to the free world very soon I familiar familiar with the town to, but I really want to give

Fig. 91

From the graphologist's report: This writer has a great need to maintain his self-image as a unique and powerful individual. Note the reversed I, flourished i-dots and unusually incised pressure. In spite of this brave front, slowness and retouching indicate a disturbed personality.

From the psychologist's report: Sociopathic personality disturbance with dyssocial and antisocial patterns. He is unstable and has ideas of persecution. His social concepts are of poor quality . . . intolerant of all authority.

Chapter 12

YOUR CREATIVITY

Do you know whether you belong in the category labeled "creative"? The way you write offers a clue.

Webster's Dictionary defines creativity as the ability to cause something unique to come into being.

We are accustomed to think of artists, writers, composers and poets, as creative people. They do "bring into being" unique creations: paintings, novels, music and poetry. But the creative category covers much more than the arts; it includes innovative businessmen, administrators, professional people—even persons who work at very ordinary routine jobs but possess more than spectator interest in creative living.

Creating your own writing form is part of normal development. Maturation involves the ability to do as we wish with positive results. Writing, also, involves this concept. We first write as we are taught—then as we wish.

If you are highly creative in many areas, you have a remarkable talent for perceiving relationships. This talent is reflected in an unconscious awareness of the three writing zones and the use of short-cuts between them. The ability to write easily throughout all three writing zones suggests a life-style operating in an expedient and perhaps non-conforming manner. Awareness of pattern, time and motion is expressed by simplified and condensed writing gestures. Recognizing the importance of getting down to fundamentals is an essential quality of the writer with a simplified style. Tri-zonal dynamics are expressed by simplifying letters with extensions such as f, g, h, y, and the capitals.

Fig. 92

Creative balancing of new forms, as in Figure 92, is most often found in the handwriting of gifted persons. Balancing or integrating your *I* in an original but natural manner says something about the writer's approach to problem-solving. A rhythmic, synergized movement suggests a progressive, adaptable attitude. Your ability to communicate with others is suggested by how ornately or how simply you choose to write. Difficulty in communicating may be suspected when the writer over-embellishes his ego symbol—as in Figure 93—or, at the other extreme, fragments it.

Fig. 93

Full access to one's creative potential presupposes a certain amount of freedom from anxiety, for anxiety is crippling to the creative process. The inner self needs to be free and to find the courage to be imperfect—it must have a wide selection of choices of action. The neurotic individual with his limited and rigid view of what is "correct" or "proper" curtails his own creativity.

In handwriting two factors characterize creativity: First, the move away from copybook models in a perceptive and original manner; second, the use of simplified movements within the total writing.

Forming the capital *I* in the school model, or copybook, fashion is not a simple motion. Copybook, or merely pretty, handwriting is often an indication of lack of creativity on the part of the writer. Departures from the early school-model, on the other hand, can be indicators of the gifted person.

A simplified writing style is evident when copybook action is abandoned in favor of the direct approach. Such writing often reveals a determined and single-minded attitude toward the self which may be the beginning of creative endeavors. Turning the series of loops into a straight line is the opposite of complexity, intricacy and division into parts. Such simplicity may be termed sophisticated when the entire writing is pared down and embellishments such as ornate loops are modified.

This quality of simplicity is a neutral factor which can be used in a negative or positive manner. The sociopath may write a simplified *I*, suggesting a commitment to himself at the expense of other people. The artist may also write an *I* in a straight line, indicating devotion to his creative self. The final evaluation of simplicity depends upon what the term means to the writer. It is generally the sign of a complicated personality who has the facility to create unusual things or situations. Causes and consequences of this simplicity are multiple.

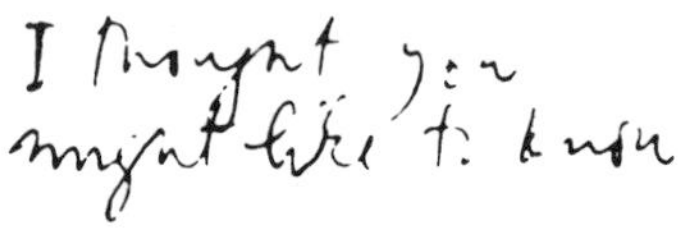

Fig. 94

The unusual and simplified forms in all zones in Figure 94 affirm the creative writer. He is a young poet who enjoys all the arts. High level writing characterizes his productive and independent pp*I*.

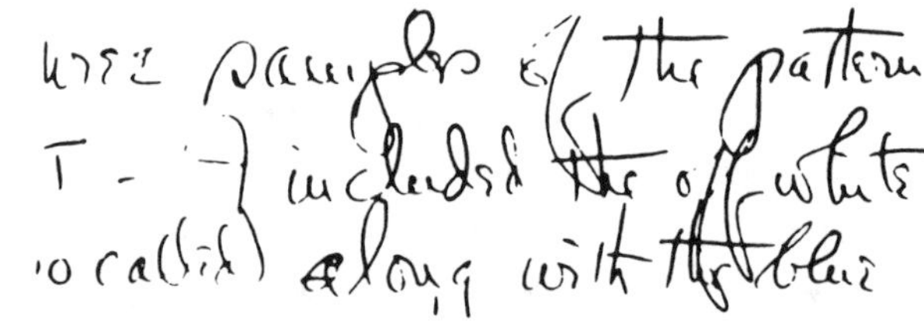

Fig. 95

The writer of Figure 95 owns her own exclusive wallpaper and paint shop as well as a boutique. A good businesswoman, she is creatively involved in management and customer relations. Her simplified *I*, heavy pressure, and crowded writing speak of a busy life.

Whatever the reasons for the original *I*, the writer is expressing himself in a somewhat detached manner.

Harmonious or inharmonious conditions may have precipitated such writing action. The writer perceives the essentials of his needs in an uncommon manner. A printed or simple line *I* often reveals a need on the part of the writer to remain aloof and unencumbered by the demands of conventional society.

Another clue to creativity is found in the writer's selection of a pen. If he is particularly sensitive to form, design, color and texture, he often selects a blunt-pointed or felt-tipped pen. The heavier stroke left on the paper is termed "pastose" and may appeal to the writer's sense of control, vitality and personal sensuousness. Artists and designers frequently select a writing instrument because of its rich tactile quality.

When the refined, delicate line is emphasized through a choice of a thin-lined, sharply pointed pen tip, the writer's interest in detail may be suspected. In both instances, the fact that extremes of linear perception are emphasized by the writer suggests there may be some appreciation of creativity or inclination toward the arts.

Fig. 96

The writer of Figure 96 is an artist. She is noted for her fine portraits. An unusually formed pp*I* indicates her interest in line and pattern. She is adept at design and color and uses her pen with the same fluency and richness that characterizes her art work.

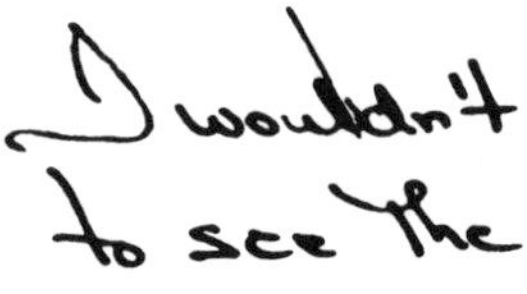

Fig. 97

The distinctive script of the young woman who wrote Figure 97 speaks of her interest and ability in the field of interior design. Shapes and textures are particularly appealing to her, as suggested by her pastose writing and graceful pp*I*.

Fig. 98

The pp*I* in Figure 98 reflects the writer's vivid imagination and personal ambitions. She is a young woman who is interested in both art history—her chosen field—and political issues. Her motivation and aspirations are shown by the enlarged loop of her ego symbol. She has a strong desire for personal growth and expanded horizons.

Simplification of line is often a declaration of independence and may symbolize a break with traditions. Any loop retards forward writing motion; therefore, in essence, straight lines are no-nonsense and may indicate a particular need for action. The straight strokes of the well-formed Roman numeral I, for instance, suggest that you see yourself as an independent person who needs freedom and wants to do things in your own way. You visualize yourself as a doer, an achiever who brings about new changes.

Determining whether the simplicity which the writer brings to the world is positive and of value to him is accomplished by carefully comparing the *I* with the rest of the handwriting. One may use the term "profoundly simple" in cases where the writing as a whole is in keeping with the pp*I*, as well as being both fluid and spontaneous.

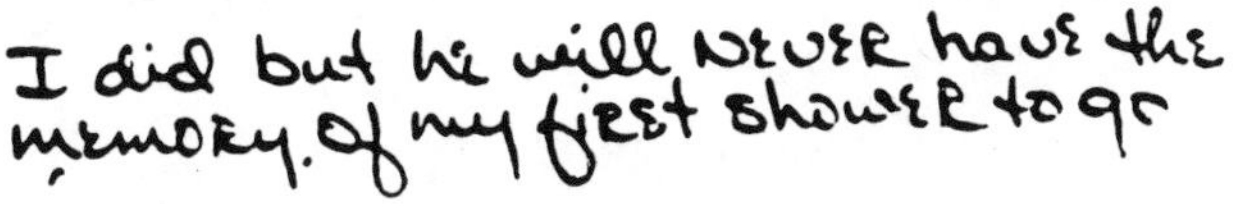

I did but he will NEVER have the memory. of my first shower to go

Fig. 99

The young woman who wrote Figure 99 is a teacher of journalism. She is also adept in the field of art and involved with potterymaking, weaving and building her own home—a talented entrepeneur.

The writer of Figure 100 is a careful businessman who is the head of his own company. He is also an author. His talents are multi-faceted, as the originality of his writing forms indicates. Sharpness of stroke is in keeping with a keen and always active mind. Although he is an elderly gentleman, the control and fluency of his handwriting belong to youth. The upper zone loop of his personal pronoun suggests a lively imagination and interest in ideas. Naturalness, aesthetic balance in the use of space, good organization, rhythm and firmness of ductus all contribute to the high form level of this writing.

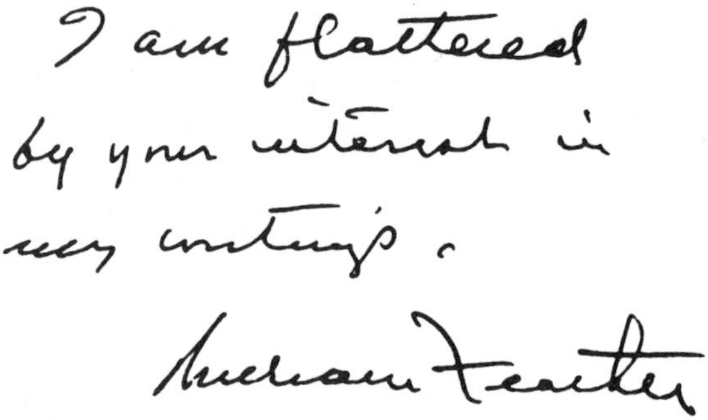

Fig. 100

The larger-than-life handwriting of designer Donald Brooks in Figure 101 is in harmony with a dynamic and gifted individual who likes structured patterns and is impatient with slowness. He has a great capacity for observation and spontaneity. He is a free spirit who respects achievement in himself and others. The upright slant suggests self-control that may be the secret to his resiliency. The writer's artistry and creativity are suggested by the original writing form, simplicity and fluency. The textured quality of the almost painted ductus reflects his highly developed perceptual appreciation. The independent pp*I* is both simple and elaborated. In spite of his social adeptness the writer is not easily known. He is a

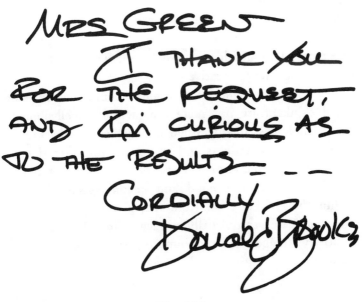

Fig. 101

noticeable and complex person with a deep commitment to the arts.

In summary, creative writing may appear as varied to the untrained eye as one creative person is from another; what is common to the creative bent is an individualistic attitude freely expressing itself. Four traits *psychologically* evaluated as characterizing creative thinking are fluency, flexibility, originality and elaboration on stereotyped ideas. Handwriting ranking high in these categories may be equated with the creative individual. Such writing may not appear pretty—it may be considered unruly, crowded, even distorted, by its originator. This, however, may correlate with the creative need and tolerance for a certain amount of disorder, particularly during a crisis of creative endeavor. Disjointedness, breaks between letters or syllables suggest the creative pause.

The graphic elaborations found within the writings of gifted thinkers are not mere ornamental embellishment, but at their best distinguished by balance and harmony. Spontaneity, naturalness and expressiveness are reflected in creative graphic strokes. New forms are structured and redefined within the mind and become visible in part within the writing trail. Rounded, pictorial-type writing often indicates the visually-minded writer. Whatever the creativity, the personal pronoun *I* represents a vivid part of its making.

Chapter 13

YOUR PUBLIC SIGNATURE AND YOUR PRIVATE *I*

Although the signature stands alone—just as the personal pronoun *I* stands alone—the symbolic function of each is quite different. The signature may be compared to the man awake, dreaming of possibilities. The *I* may be compared to the man asleep, unconsciously experiencing himself. Both are aspects of the total personality. Interior as well as exterior aspects are reflected in each.

As a calling-card symbol of yourself, written for an audience, the way you write your name may or may not be compatible with your inner estimation, as was illustrated by the case of Fred D. in chapter 2. All of us have experimented with various ways of signing our names before finding what we consider an acceptable public image. Teen-agers, particularly, experiment with their names, sometimes changing the spelling, and always seeking some measure of individuality.

As ego-awareness develops, your signature becomes similar to a trademark. It may exist for legal, professional, artistic or romantic reasons. A valid graphological profile is theoretically not possible without the signature, which

141

puts the finishing touch on your self-image.

The written *I* is so much a part of you as a person that it is written much more naturally than the signature and is much less subject to deliberate tamperings. The writer who does seek to change his pp*I* consciously must be an exceptionally ego-aware individual. An unusual desire to manipulate himself toward certain goals is thereby expressed. Because the *I* is linked subjectively to personal imagination, it is generally less objective than your signature.

The signature is concerned not only with the public, but with the family. For example, psychotherapy has shown unconscious factors to be at work when a newly married woman habitually forgets to sign her married name.

Fig. 102

Graphological differences between first and last names suggest emotional differences concerning them on the writer's part. The writer who emphasizes his family name through size or spacing may feel that his first name is less significant than his family name. Strong influence on the paternal side may be implied when the accent falls on the last name as in Figure 102.

Fig. 103

Cutting back through the signature as in Figure 103, suggests a wish for independence from family tradition or family name.

Fig. 104

A covered-up signature, like the one in Figure 104, suggests a need for secrecy and dislike or hesitancy toward being known.

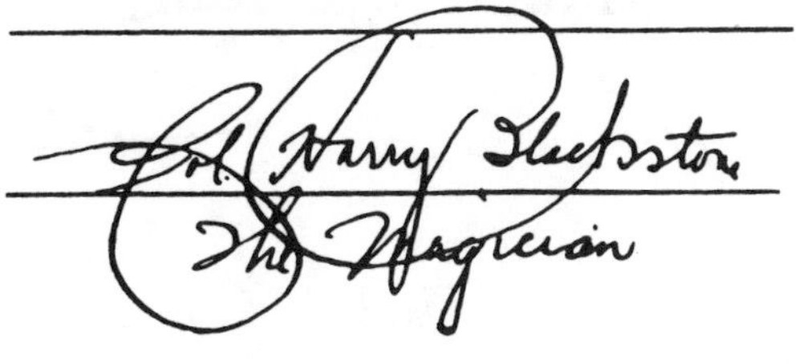

Fig. 105

Intertwined and flourished signatures suggest a liking for attention and perhaps intrigue. Arcade encirclements usually imply some defensiveness on the writer's part concerning his public image, as does the fenced-in stroke in Figure 105.

Special touches, such as underscoring the name, put the final touch upon the public image which the writer wishes to convey. A period after the name, as in Figure 106 on the next page, may indicate the writer's interest in detail.

Fig. 106

Creative persons often embellish their signature in a distinctive fashion like Jayne Mansfield whose decorative signature is shown in Figure 107.

Fig. 107

Compare Your Signature to Your Private I: Are They In Harmony?

- *Your Responsiveness: Slant* which is the same both in the signature and the pp*I* suggests lack of conflict between your public and private image.

- *Your Self-Assurance:* When the relative *size* is equal, there is little discrepancy between your

- *Your Future Outlook: Placement* of the signature to the right, matching the right-tending personal pronoun, indicates a unified view.

- *Your Cooperative Nature:* Is all it appears to be when letter formations are similar.

- *Your Energy (psychic and physical):* Equal depth of *pressure* suggests healthy balance.

- *Your Sense of Purpose:* Is in harmony when the public signature and the pp*I* are written at the same rate of *speed* and letter style.

**Compare Your Signature and Your Private I:
Are They In Conflict?**

Will the *real* John Doe stand up?

- *Conflicting slant*

- *Conflicting size*

- *Conflicting formation*

[handwriting samples: "I am" and "John Doe" in two styles]

- *Conflicting pressure*

[handwriting samples: "I am" and "John Doe" in two styles]

- *Conflicting speed and style*

[handwriting sample: "I am John Doe"]

In the following are some signatures which you may recognize. Note the relationship between the signature and the pp*I*.

Joseph Nicolas Nicollet

Scientist-historian Joseph Nicolas Nicollet penned the missive in Figure 108 in 1841, shortly before he died at 51. Note the precision of his sharp, small writing. This brilliant scholar came to America after the French Revolution. His

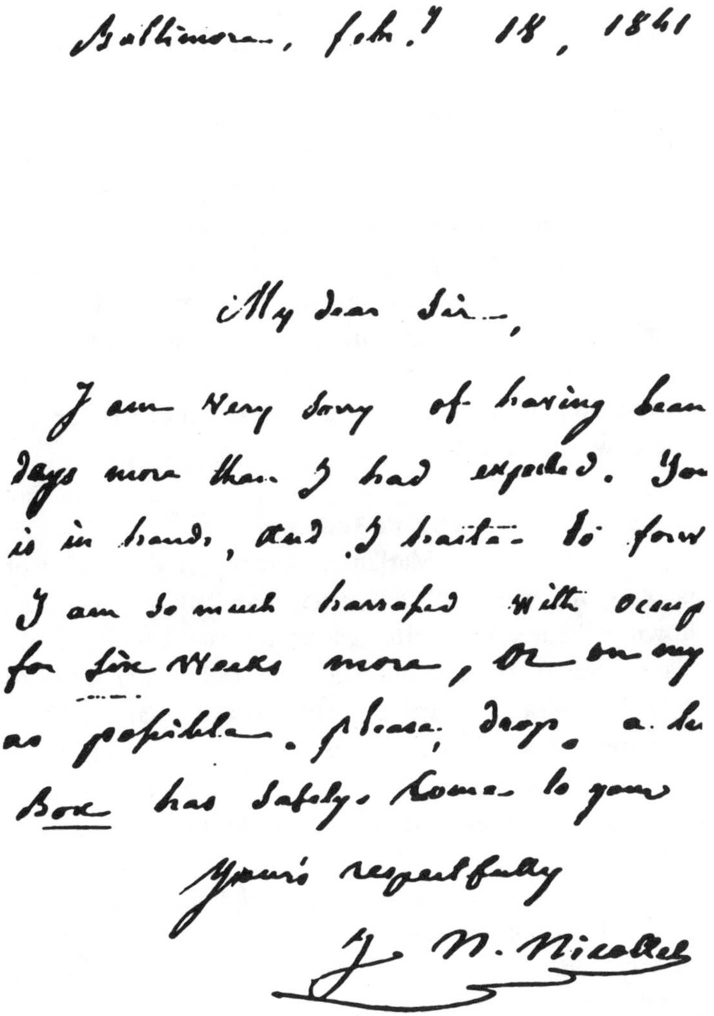

Baltimore, feb.ʸ 18, 1841

My dear Sir —,

*I am Very sorry of having been
days more than I had expected. You
is in hands, and I hesita- to forw
I am so much harrased with occup
for six Weeks more, or on my
as possible. please, deop, a le
Box has safely. come to your*

Yours respectfully

J. N. Nicollet

Fig. 108

official report and map of the hydrographic basin on the upper Mississippi has been called one of the most important contributions ever made to American geography.

Over one hundred years later, we note his handwriting's excellent form level, creative structures and varying pp*I*'s. The first of his personal pronouns is the French J: Nicollet was first and foremost a Frenchman. The following three ego symbols vary in structure: he was writing in a new language at the time of physical and emotional stress. The signature echoes the modesty as well as a sense of distinction which he maintained. The underscoring is not unusual, and rather modest, for the time in which he lived.

Marian Anderson

The great singer Marian Anderson makes a point of speaking of herself as "we" rather than "I:" her signature, shown in Figure 109, reflects a deep awareness of self and relationship to those around her, as well as her sense of obligation. Note the upflung capitals and final stroke of her name, which flies into the upper area of ethical and spiritual considerations. Since her retirement, this honored musician has been active in a wide range of service activities.

Strong pressure, large size, disciplined attention to detail all speak of the writer's determination. She is actively dedicated to all in which she believes and has a singular capacity for hard work. Note the extra firm i dots: Marian Anderson is a careful observer. Her angular and graceful writing speaks of control and methodical attention.

The scope of her signature is in keeping with the

writing above it. Underlining her signature echoes this writer's sense of mission.

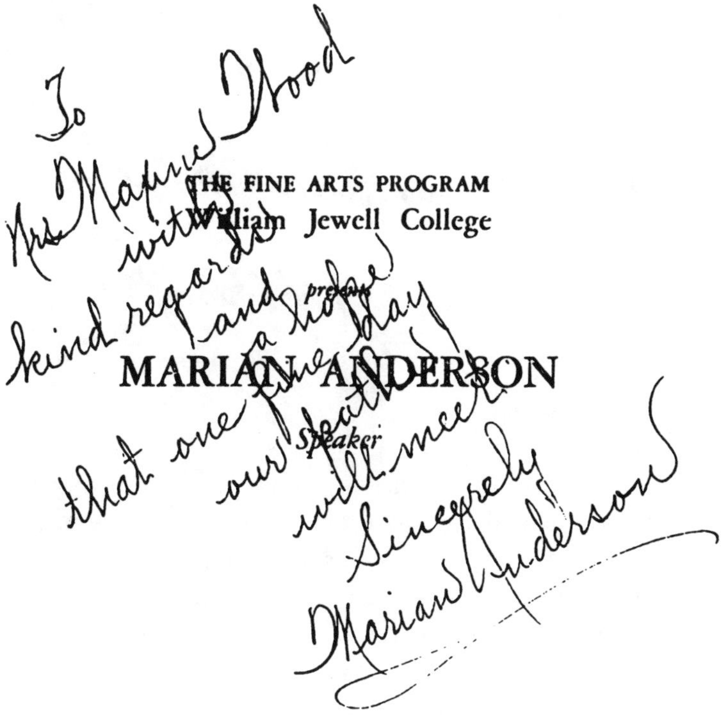

Fig. 109

Hubert Humphrey

The large writing of former Vice-President Hubert Humphrey, shown in Figure 110, moves across the paper with force and spontaneity, just as the writer moves in public and private life. The rightward slant and generous size emphasize his enthusiastic nature. He is interested in large issues, plans and enterprises. Closely spaced small letters denote a need to relate to others.

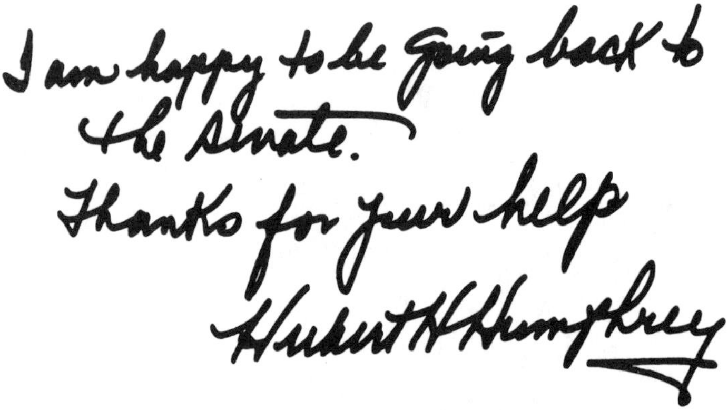

Fig. 110

The signature is placed toward the right margin, signifying the writer's interest in future goals. The heavy pressure and good rhythm denote intense drive and emotional memory: images and recollections from the past remain potent forces in his life-style. His angled strokes express strong convictions and appreciation of hard-work. He thinks accurately and quickly, as the well-detailed and speedy script emphasizes. Superior executive ability is shown in the simple manner he connects the capitals in his signature.

The private *I* of Mr. Humphrey is less noticeable than his signature. Its moderate size and scope reveal a man of practical outlook and good adjustment to circumstances. The sharp top of his *I* conveys quick perception. His innate restlessness is tempered inwardly by a sensitivity and caution which may seem at variance with his written public image. He is not as impulsive as his signature suggests—the *I* is not slanted, but vertical, indicating some effort on the writer's part to hold himself back for thoughtful consideration. A lack of personal vanity is affirmed by this modestly formed ego symbol. Angles within its structure speak of energy and will-power which absorbs tension.

John F. Kennedy

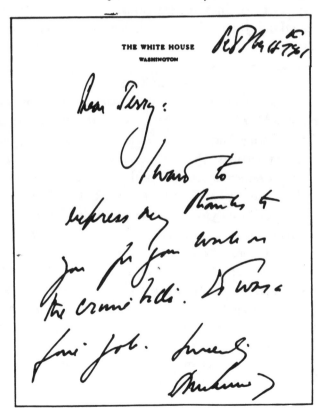

Fig. 111

The dynamic nature of John F. Kennedy's quick writing in Figure 111 echoes his personality. A creative mixture of thread, angles, arcades and garlands testify to his versatility. The upward swing is characteristic of a person who knows few boundaries. Heavy pressure and distinctive, simplified *I* emphasize the writer's involvement in out-of-the-ordinary pursuits: two small hooks embellish his ego symbol. The writer likes to acquire new ideas and is persistent in his convictions. The *I* is vertically space-taking. John Kennedy enjoyed the heights to which he aspired.

Arthur King

Arthur King is a creative jeweler known both here and abroad for jewelry conceived in unique forms. He is an artist at fitting baroque pearls and other unusual gems in sculptured settings. He uses his signature as a hallmark in his advertisements. Seeing both signature and jewelry together, the graphologist is struck by their similar pattern: both are dynamic, movement-laden forms.

Arthur King is a thread writer, as his signature reveals vividly in Figure 112. He is impatient with the status-quo and slowness, and bound by no rules so far as his unique talents go. He is totally engrossed by his art—even his small i-dot is a ring. The pastose, rich line of his writing expresses the writer's appreciation of design, texture and color. It has a sensuous quality of its own.

The *I* of this artist is as creative as himself, and in perfect accord with his simplified writing. The straight line

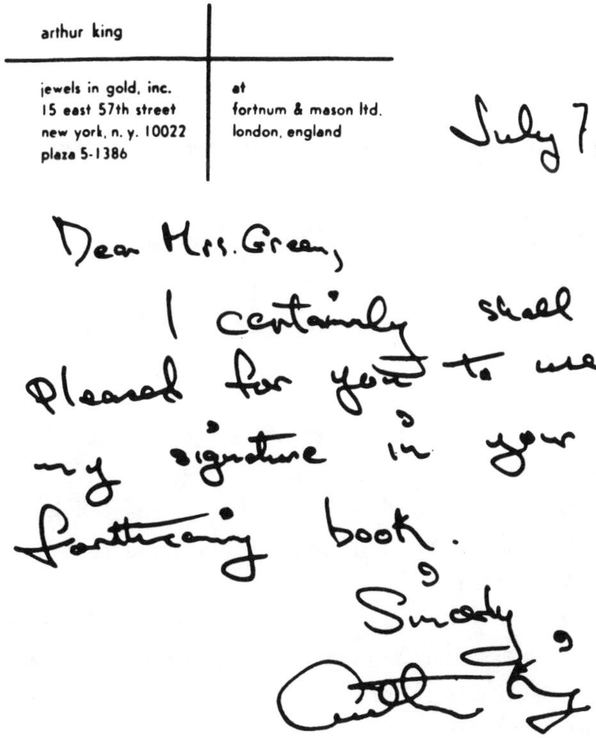

arthur king

jewels in gold, inc.	at
15 east 57th street	fortnum & mason ltd.
new york, n. y. 10022	london, england
plaza 5-1386	

July 7,

Dear Mrs. Green,

I certainly shall be pleased for you to use my signature in your forthcoming book.

Sincerely

[signature]

Fig. 112

has a tiny hook at its top, barely discernible, but nevertheless quite definite. Mr. King has firm notions concerning aesthetic and philosophic values. Discriminating taste and individuality are elements of his personality. The tallness of his ego symbol conveys pride and confidence, independence and a persistent desire to express himself.

Reverend Barbara L. Andrews

> *Conflict is an inevitable characteristic of both institutional and personal relationships. It can be positive and creative; it can also be negative and destructive. Ideally, conflict is a force for growth wherever it is found.*
>
> *Rev. Barbara L. Andrews*

Fig. 113

Reverend Barbara L. Andrews is the first ordained woman minister in the American Lutheran Church. She suffered a birth injury and is confined to a wheelchair. In spite of her disability, her writing reveals she is not handicapped in spirit.

It takes this young woman much time and effort to write; nevertheless, her handwriting in Figure 113 shows comparatively little tremor or disintegration, because of her control and carefulness.

The moderate signature indicates modesty mixed with persistence and tenacity. The writer suppresses emotions and ideas which are negative and moves ahead to meet all challenges. The precision and painstaking qualities within the script point to her attention to detail. This is predominantly garland writing—Reverend Andrews enjoys people and is receptive to new ideas. She is embarking upon a ministry to the physically disabled within her church which should bring hope to many persons. Such remarkably controlled handwriting in one who has a disability can belong only to one who controls herself remarkably.

PART II

MALE-FEMALE SYMBOLISM WITHIN THE I

Chapter 1

BACKGROUND OF THE SEXUAL SELF

Just as the private self-image reflects a person's previous experiences, we may assume that the expressive movements of his handwriting reflect something of his background environment, that they incorporate the most intimate experience of beginning life: the family unit. According to contemporary behavioral scientists, interpersonal relationships within the family are significant determiners of ultimate ego strength.

In forming the pp*I*, certain strokes appear in some form to revive a situation of which the writer was originally a part. It seems reasonable that the writing of so personal a gesture as the ego-symbol may offer some clues to the total response once made to the parental figures or their surrogates. Counterparts of earlier responses may also be found in later everyday male-female relationships.

The psychiatrist Alfred Adler has pointed out that the infant's relationship with its mother is the first social training received by the human being: myriad possibilities and aptitudes are developed when the infant begins to relate to his mother. Existing in social relationships from

157

birth on, the individual's awareness of and receptivity to others has its base in the family unit.

The *I* you write is expressive of the principle that you are continually relating to others even when you believe you are most intimately committed to yourself. Like parts of a puzzle, the central factors of personality shown by the pp*I* fit intelligibly together. Your ego symbol may contain not only the overall gestalt of the self-image, but also segments within its form offering hints as to your innermost feelings concerning male and female and how you may choose to identify with or relate to them.

Identification appears to be vital in the growing-up process whereby you begin to accept your identity as a male or a female as a way of life. To identify with another means basically to model or copy yourself after someone. It usually incorporates empathy with another, including feelings of sympathy, affection and respect. The identification of a girl with her mother appears to play a large role in her ability later to accept herself as a woman; the identification of a boy with his father is important in establishing his concept of what it means to grow up into a man.

How the individual regards himself or herself in being male or female appears to be crucial in establishing satisfactory heterosexual relationships. The full development of personality includes making decisions, largely unconscious, regarding how you will act toward persons of your own and the opposite sex. Theoretical knowledge of these delicate factors is constantly being explored by behavioral scientists; however, research is at present still inconclusive.

One parent alone does not play a total role in the individual's identification, for both parent figures interact and affect relationships. What we consider "feminine" or "masculine" is as much culturally as biologically determined. Mothers in our culture who are warm, affectionate and rewarding with their girls appear likely to have daughters who are not feminine-rejecting; masculine-acting boys appear generally to have fathers who are good models of men—patient, powerful and able to reward their sons easily, as well as punish them when needed.

Normally, each parent will personify to the child what is meant by *male* and *female*. From his observations, the child will interpret and internalize attitudes about himself and others. These earliest attitudes will be reflected to some extent in the most intimate communication of all—that of sexual experience. The parent may be replaced by a guardian or some other surrogate; nevertheless, through such role models, the child finds personal meanings about himself or herself as a boy or girl which offer a pattern for later sexual development and expression.

Multiple shades of meaning exist in all aspects of identifying with another human being. There is no simple formula; psychologically, there are cross-identifications which help the female understand the male point of view, and vice-versa. Your written *I* cannot be the total story of the self. However, its shape offers clues to your sexual feelings and attitudes.

Such reactions have in some measure been related to the self-image. For instance, a small boy may have been overly controlled by his mother and always felt the need for a strong male relationship. As an adult, he may fear and reject domineering women, or have difficulty in establishing a relationship which does not unduly threaten him.

A small girl with a poor father relationship may develop grave doubts as to her worth as a female. These uncertainties about her self-image may create sexual problems for her later. Such a person may seek total independence from males, or perhaps be inclined to relate comfortably only to men who will exploit her.

With these factors in mind, the working hypothesis is established that the copybook Zaner-Blozer or Palmer type pp*I* contains both male and female symbols within its formation. This hypothesis rests on many case histories, counseling and follow-up questionnaires. According to the hypothesis, the writer's identification with the parental authority figures as well as his relationship with these figures may be expressed by his written *I*. The dominant parental authority figure may also be evidenced in the written *I*. The term "dominant" refers to the parental figure (male or female) who appears most relevant to the writer in making decisions affecting him.

Chapter 2

WHAT DOES "FEMALE" MEAN TO YOU?

The mother figure is important to each of us on all three levels of communication—physical, mental, emotional. She represents the great experience of beginning love and fellowship. She is so important to an infant that if deserted, he may sicken and die, even with adequate custodial care. Studies show that children thus abandoned are apt to be more fearful and generally below average in overall development. Living together, mother and child receive nourishment, both physical and emotional. The very word "mothering" connotes protective, affectionate behavior toward the helpless. The give-and-take of social relationships is within the circular response from one to the other, as mother and child become a unit.

The circular embrace of the mother figure relates to softness, which is symbolically and psychologically opposed to hardness, represented by angled or straight lines. The circle and loop have been regarded as having special properties throughout civilizations which have come and gone. The magic circle around the altar, the concept of the solar system itself, find affinity with all of us.

Small children draw circles to represent themselves or the entirety of anything. The circle embraces the concept of the "all." Its symbolic relation to protection, an encirclement of all, is apparent. In the ego symbol, such a circular stroke has a symbolic significance—not only with regard to the self—but also with regard to the writer's relationship with the male and female authority figures.

We would expect to find symbols of the mother figure within the total framework of the *I*, in all three handwriting zones. This is the case in copybook writing, since the *I* begins in the lower zone: the starting point slightly below the baseline is a symbol of the self beginning from the unconscious level of physical being.

The writer proceeds into the middle zone, harnessing his physical instincts and unconscious impulses into an upward movement. He now proceeds leftward: movement to the left, as stated before, expresses the reaching backwards into past experience. It symbolizes a measure of security and offers protection, a summing-up of resources before movement to the opposite right begins.

Going beyond the middle zone—the area of reality—the writer moves into the upper area of the abstract and ideal. Symbolism of height embraces not only the concept of power; it also emphasizes concepts of virtue or holiness. Just as the mother figure includes a sense of loftiness, so such sheltering curved motion implies both historical and mythical assumptions of sheltering, nurturing motherhood.

Upon reaching the end of the upper zone stroke, the writer proceeds in a curving motion to the right: this motion of flexibility and yielding qualities suggests culturally accepted aspects of feminine behavior.

The size is in good proportion to the continuing stroke which enters the lower middle zone and begins the symbol of the father figure.

All these factors are established within the framework of the written pp*I*. Visions of the ideal mother or female authority figure lie above and beyond the daily routine, yet rooted in those aspects of living which surround each of us.

Chapter 3

WHAT DOES "MALE" MEAN TO YOU?

"My father can beat your father," has long been a battle cry to establish domination. Children of both sexes appear inclined to regard their dad as a model of strength and courage, if they possibly can. While peaceable action is a hallmark of the feminine, the masculine counterpart is traditionally rough and tough, a hero figure to the small fry eager to identify with the aggressor.

The legendary male encompasses the idea of action within the everyday world, and we associate the idea of the male with someone who seeks to extend his power in an active and dynamic manner. The traditional passivity of the female is complemented and supported by the active, vigorous male figure. Male drive and energy, power and bravery are even exemplified through such terms as "fatherland" which has historically been used by aggressive nations. From primordial times, motherhood has implied the sheltering and nurturing aspects of life, just as fatherhood has implied the supplying and defending aspects. Father figures are thus oriented toward progress with all of its social, economic and practical considerations.

165

The working father may also provide the child with a sense of the importance of the world beyond the home.

Because the daily actions of society are found graphologically within the middle zone, this area is symbolically correlated with the male figure, beginning (in the copybook form) with a continuing leftward-moving stroke and running in a slight curve along the baseline of the middle zone. It then sweeps slightly upward until its length approximates that of the upright mother, or female, figure. Forming a sharp angle, the stroke turns back to the right and continues in dynamic fashion straight forward past the area of integration with the female symbol.

Both the male and the female figure appear balanced and harmonious in the copybook version of the *I*. Such

equality carries a literal and philosophical connotation of likeness of value, matching importance and unity. Similarity of length implies a proportionate and coordinated effort, fused at the integrated point where the two forms cross each other.

The forward stroke to the right of the father figure balances the heavier-appearing weight of the female symbol. Total configuration of the copybook *I* offers food for thought concerning a balanced and harmonious family life.

While the mother aspect of the *I* involves a curve, the father figure carries both curved and straight strokes; both the *soft* and the *hard* are contained within this figure, quite in keeping with the best aspects of the father at home and at work. A slightly curved rightward stroke instead of a straight line is sometimes employed in the copybook form; in such case, a more sharply executed angle is used, still significant of the *hard* male aspect.

Fathers of today are depended upon for emotional as well as financial support. Their attitude toward the child may run the gamut from yielding sentiment to strict authoritarianism. Both aspects play important roles in the development of healthy, well-integrated children of both sexes. In fact, the lack of a strong father figure has been called a central factor in juvenile delinquency.

Let us briefly summarize the zonal placement of the male and female authority figures in the copybook form of the pp*I* before we apply this analysis to a concrete graphological sample: The mother figure is symbolized by the vertical part of the personal pronoun encompassing all three zones—upper, middle and lower. It is perpendicular to the father figure. The father image is found in the middle zone, running horizontally to the baseline of the writing. An area of integration, or fusion, of both the male and female image lies within the base of the loops in the middle zone.

We shall now turn to a concrete example to see what graphological inferences we can draw from these relationships.

The writing in Figure 114 belongs to a member of a Clinical Pastoral Education course given at a large metropolitan teaching hospital. The students were seminarians and ministers who were receiving advanced training in counseling procedures. The course covered several months of group therapy; testing materials included the Minnesota Multiphasic Personality Inventory as well as a handwriting analysis of each participant. The writer is presently interning as a hospital chaplain:

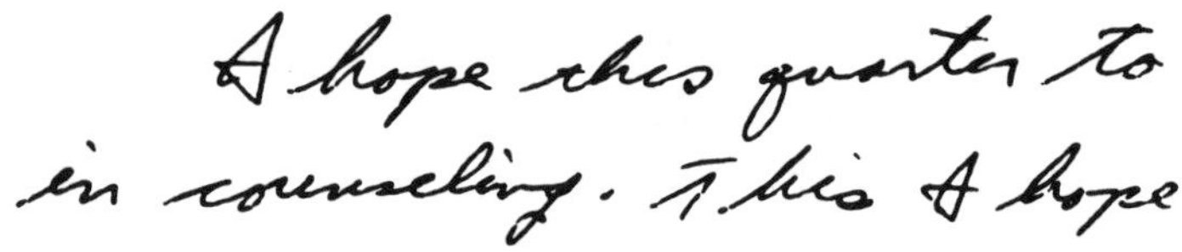

Fig. 114

His parental relations suggested by his pp*I* indicate underlying conflict, although his parents were a united pair, warm and close. The writer was emotionally closer to his mother than to his father. In his 20's, he found it necessary to virtually disown both parents for a period of time in order to establish his independence from them. Cutting the apron strings required a firm showdown.

Note that the subject's angular pp*I* is in keeping with his need for independent thinking and self-assertion. Conflict within the writer's self-concept was reflected during his adolescence when he battled shyness and deep feelings of inferiority. He was, and still is, an achiever. He graduated as valedictorian of his high school class. He later was an honors graduate engineer, involved in research for ten lucrative years before turning to the ministry. During those years, his acquisitive nature found success and satisfaction in material things.

The writer is divorced from an alcoholic for whom he appears to have been a father figure. His MMPI profile lies well within the normal range for his occupation, weighted slightly toward the feminine scale. His signature (not shown here) emphasizes his first name more than the last: this appears to be in keeping with his maternal relationship. He is outgoing and finds emotional satisfaction in building relationships with people and being of service to them.

The points of his ego symbol are echoed in the sharpness of the rest of the writing. It is interesting to note that the straight structured line of his pp*I* is typical of many engineers who print. Note, too, that the *I* is formed in the beginning shape of a star. The writer's favorite and habitual "doodle" is a five-pointed star: a star, in "doodle language" is said to represent high aims, spiritually and philosophically.

The writer is aggressive, sensitive and analytical, all indicated within the form of his written ego symbol. The hook on his pp*I* suggests his desire to acquire things which he considers valuable: at first, material possessions, later, worthwhile ego satisfaction. He is ambitious for attainment which will be meaningful to himself and to others.

The following chapters will deal with the six specific factors of male-female symbolism in the personal pronoun, presenting corroborative evidence from actual graphological studies.

There appear to be six elements which create the picture of family interpersonal relationships and represent male-female symbolism. These are height or length, slant, pressure, scope, angularity and elaboration. A single factor alone cannot tell the whole story.

The handwriting preceding each chapter offers the reader an opportunity to assess the writer's view of himself, a view expressed not only by his written words, but also by the expressive movement of his written ego symbols.

Chapter 4

HEIGHT-LENGTH AS A MALE-FEMALE FACTOR

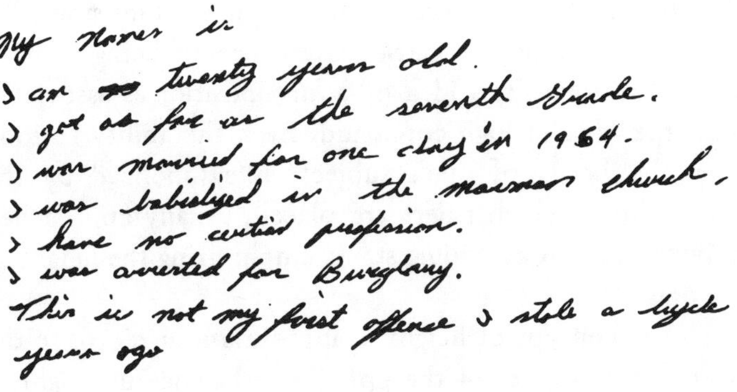

Fig. 115

The human heart seems to recognize that distance may be equated with an ideal: we do not approach greatness easily, either actually or figuratively. Effort and time are involved in approaching the heights of any endeavor. Distance does lend enchantment. The old saying, "Familiarity breeds contempt" and "No man is a hero to his valet" are recognitions that a degree of removal sustains idealization.

171

The concept of height is symbolically associated with the idea of superior worth and/or the idea of power. Height plays a part in symbolizing the admirable or sublime and is particularly significant in religious or ethical areas. Graphologically, the distance (worth) is greater, or less, depending on the distance from the everyday or mundane, symbolized in handwriting by the baseline of the middle zone.

Conversely, the symbolism for inferiority is shortness in height, manifested in both animals and humans. Kneeling or lying on the ground implies submission. The concept of authority carries overtones of being *over* or *under* someone. The idea of a *high* position is associated with the idea of high command. Even the ability to look over the heads of one's subjects is symbolized by the throne upon which rulers are placed, usually approached only by a set of ascending stairs, emphasizing the height of the dais.

The concept of height is appropriate in regard to the male-female figures of the pp*I*. Equal balance in height of the female and length of the male image is significant. Disparity in length indicates some degree of disparity in parental or male-female significance to the writer.

Unusual height within the female figure suggests private concepts connected with that symbol. Unusually long length of the male image suggests strong paternal influences on the writer: in some case the writer swings way to the left before completing the final stroke of the pp*I*.

The writer of Figure 116 is a male, age 32. The

Fig. 116

identification with his father is strong. The father was close to the writer and spent much time with him. The family was united and compatible, with a feeling of partnership in the home. (Note the harmoniously coupled parent symbols.) A conventional family group.

Fig. 117

The writer of Figure 117 is a female, age 27. She identifies strongly with her mother. Her sympathy and respect for the mother is shown by the accented female symbol. The limited stroke of the male image is reminiscent of her father who played second fiddle in a household of women.

The length and height of the male and female symbols are often conversely related. As the male symbol increases in height, the female symbol decreases in length and vice versa; if this is the case, there appears to be little question as to which parent exercised the greatest influence upon the writer.

The writer of Figure 118 is a female, age 18. Her relationship with her father is poor. She grew up in a family of academic brilliance which alienated itself from

Am going to

Fig. 118

the community. She has a deep hatred of her father and is a lesbian. Emotionally disturbed at times, she has attempted suicide. Note the lower zone father symbol with its muddiness. Her pp*I* accents the female symbol.

Within the realm of authority and leadership, the dynamic qualities of the male figure are emphasized through increased length which penetrates and passes through and beyond the female figure. Paternal influence is thereby strengthened. The length of the father figure stroke is shortened if it does not pass through the area of the mother figure, the triangular area of integration and fusion.

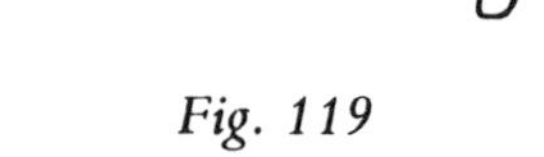

I think my

Fig. 119

The writer of Figure 119 is a female, age 20. She has a strong relationship with her parents, who were eminently compatible and established a warm home for their children. She views herself as falling short of their standards—as the shortness of her pp*I* suggests—but the firmness of her writing attests to her strong convictions. She is herself happily married.

The writer of Figure 120 is a male, age 24. His father

I believe my

Fig. 120

is the authority in the home. He has little self-confidence, as suggested by the size of his pp*I* in comparison with the rest of his writing. The home was dominated by his father who drank excessively. His parents were unified, however, in their determination to stick together. Note the integration of the male and female symbol. The writer lacks determination, as suggested by the "rocking-horse" base of his pp*I*.

If I had not

Fig. 121

The writer of Figure 121 is a male, age 23. His mother was the authority in the home. His father travelled extensively, but the mother did a good job of bringing up the children. The writer often felt that his father was the underdog and had some anxiety about his identification with him as a male. He is not married.

In general, the greater the height of the male symbol or the length of the female symbol, the stronger the desire of the writer to relate to that image. It is not the height or length alone, however, which tells the story of the self-image.

The printed pp*I* sometimes offers clues about the

writer's tendencies to identify with either the male or female authority figure. In the printed pp*I* the top is equated with the mother symbol; the bottom bar with the father symbol. The stem appears to symbolize the central factor, the self. The predominance of these factors as well as the length of the printed pp*I* will suggest the writer's proclivity to identify with either male or female figure. If the stroke is single, the self may be viewed as standing alone, independent of either figure.

All other handwriting factors must be taken into account in the complete graphological analysis. Yet, all other factors being equal, shortness of either the male or female symbol may imply difficulties in identifying with either the male or female authority figure.

Chapter 5

SLANT AS A MALE-FEMALE FACTOR

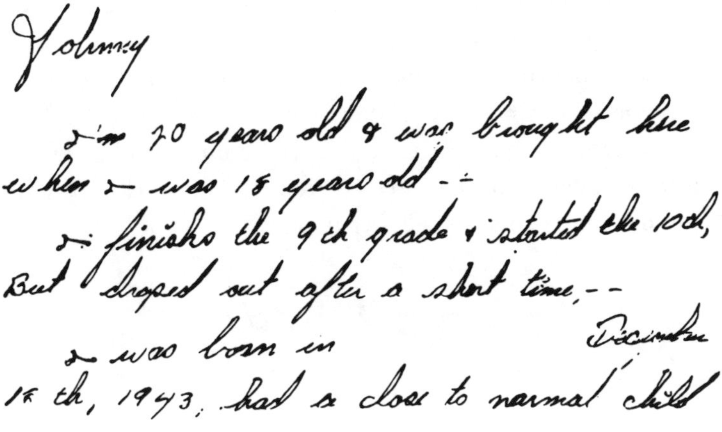

Johnny

I'm 70 years old & was brought here
when I was 18 years old. -
I finished the 9th grade & started the 10th,
But dropped out after a short time, --
I was born in December
18th, 1943, had a close to normal child

Fig. 122

The chosen slant of writing may be influenced by whim or style. It takes more than casual observance to determine the most natural slant of the writing. In determining slant, right- or left- handedness must be taken into account. Left-handed writers find it easier under certain circumstances to write with a left or vertical slant; therefore the analyst must know the physical basis for

177

unusual slanting before deciding upon its significance.

The Leftward pp*I*

The leftward pp*I* points the way not to *you* but to *me*. If the *I* is slanted toward the left, an inference of defensiveness can be made. There are probably as many reasons for feeling defensive as there are persons feeling that way. One of them may lie with the mother figure, particularly if that area of the *I* is unusually bent.

Broadly speaking, if the writer is female, such leftward bending may suggest a feeling of concern toward the self. Identification with the mother may be tinged with pity or worry because of the female's secondary place in the home. If the writer of the left slanted *I* is male, we may wonder if he chooses to identify more closely with the mother than with the father figure.

I don't mean

Fig. 123

The writer of Figure 123 is a woman, age 37. Her relationship with the father was good. She comes from a broken family. Dissension and opposition have plagued her own marriage. She feels her mother was put down a great deal. (Note tiny, hung-over female figure.) The father was dominant and related well to his daughter. She dislikes male domination. She is a creative person.

The writer of Figure 124 is a young woman, age 20. Her relationship with her parents is poor. Her lack of

I think parent

Fig. 124

self-confidence is suggested by the backward motion of the *I*, as well as by the constricted movement of the female symbol. She has been criticized severely by her mother most of her life; her father has paid little attention to her.

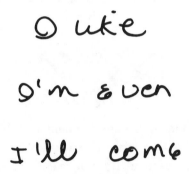

I like

I'm even

I'll come

Fig. 125

Traditionally, the left field of the writing paper is equated with the maternal. Writers of the left-slanted pp*I* may yearn for protection or comfort. This is indicated by Figure 125, the writing of a 20-year-old college student who lost her mother when she was eleven. The circular, left-tending motion of her ego symbol strongly implies dependency or a need for mothering. In such writing there is undue emphasis on the female aspects of the self. Note the changes in the writing as she grows older and more independent.

In general, it can be said that the ego symbol which slants to the left when the rest of the script moves rightward indicates some feeling of isolation or loneliness in spite of outgoing social activities. The man who wrote

Fig 126

Figure 126 was an only child raised by a widow. He never married and still lives with his mother.

Fig. 127

Opposition to the environment may be characteristic of the writer with a leftward slant within the ego symbol. This becomes particularly noticeable when the leftward slant encompasses the male figure which is not normally slanted in a particular direction. The writer of Figure 127 is a male, age 21, who has not enjoyed normal male relationships in his home.

The Upright *I*

The upright *I* points the way to "Let me do it." The writer choosing this slant is inclined toward neither parent. A need to find his own way in life seems to be uppermost in his mind. While this aloofness may be forced, it generally indicates the writer's will-power. The writer of such a balanced ego symbol seeks equilibrium in his parental relationships and may have a strong need for harmony as well as privacy.

Nevertheless, the writer who seeks independence from his parents will usually have some small indications in the *I* to show his natural emotional responses: these are to be found within the total six factors concerning the male-female symbols.

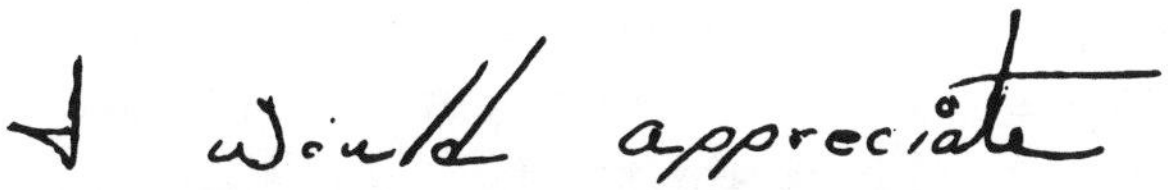

Fig. 128

The writer of Figure 128 is a male, age 30. His relationship with his parents was poor. He is hostile and aggressive, lacking ability to relate easily or deeply to most people. His family life was not harmonious; he shows tension and a need to feel superior in his angular, tall, upright personal pronoun.

Fig. 129

The upright slant of the printed ego symbol in Figure 129 reveals independence and the writer's need for self-assertion. (The lower bar is habitually written with the most emphasis—the writer was obviously a daddy's girl.)

The Rightward *I*

The rightward *I* points the way to "free and easy." The writer of the rightward ego symbol is not neutral in his feelings toward the male-female symbols within his pp*I*. His feelings will be intensified by the rightward movement, expressing emotionality. Generally, we find that the more natural or average the slant of the *I*, the more freely the writer can respond to parental figures.

According to traditional European graphology right-tending movements symbolize the father, as well as the future, and progressive movement toward a goal. Rightward slant therefore carries some symbolical connotation with regard to the writer's interest in or acceptance of male leadership.

Fig. 130

The writer of Figure 130 is a woman, age 45. Her relationship with the parents was excellent. She matured in a warm, supportive family where there was unity and respect for one another. She is a conventional person, as her preference for the school-form *I* suggests. Her father influenced her strongly (note firm terminal stroke to the right). The mother was secure and happy in her role as wife. She is a stable, outgoing person, comfortable in her role as a woman, wife and mother.

Excessive slanting to the right may have a negative connotation, as has been suggested in earlier chapters. Such

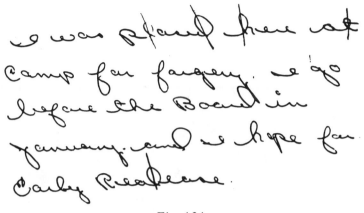

Fig. 131

supine relaxing suggests a writer who cannot say "no," who is apt to take a dare, and who does not like overt conflict. A running away is implied, with excessive vulnerability to the male authority figure. The sample in Figure 131 was written by a repeater in prison who finds it difficult to stand up for his rights and to maintain himself. Poor family relationships are evident in his handwriting.

Chapter 6

PRESSURE AS A MALE-FEMALE FACTOR

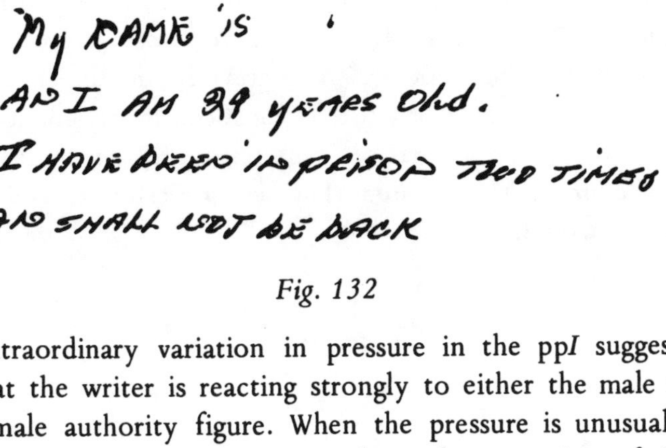

Fig. 132

Extraordinary variation in pressure in the pp*I* suggests that the writer is reacting strongly to either the male or female authority figure. When the pressure is unusually deep or dug into the paper, the violent reaction of the writer toward some parental figure involved may be suspected, just as excessive pressure on the ego symbol as a whole may convey the writer's excitability or stubbornness.

The writer of Figure 133 is a male, age 51. His

Fig. 133

mother was the dominant parent in the family. The tallness of his printed *I* (12 mm compared to an average of 7 mm in other upper zone letters) suggests pride of accomplishment. The heavy pressure (embossed on the other side) shows strong emotional recall, rightward slant, quick reactions and emotionality. Wide spacing between words suggests control and dislike of intimacy. The extra pressure and length of the upper horizontal stroke (mother figure) tells us that the household most likely was dominated by the mother. As he grew up, the subject was closer to his father. His written *I* most commonly connects the lower horizontal stroke (male image) to the stem; the female image is separated. The writer prefers to isolate himself from her.

Fig. 134

The writer of Figure 134 is a female, age 20. Her relationship with her father was good. She comes from a conservative family of community leaders. Her father and mother are united in their efforts, with the father making most of the important decisions. The writer enjoys companionship with males more than with females. Note extra heavy writing pressure on the male image.

Fig. 135

The writer of Figure 135 is a male, age 20. His self-image is poor and so is his relationship with his parents. A battered child, this writer has emotional difficulties stemming from his abnormal home environment. His father was a brutal alcoholic; his mother inclined toward promiscuity. He depends on liquor and sex to provide excitement, as his generally blobby, pasty writing suggests. The undue pressure on both the male and female symbol suggests tension and rage. He has attempted both murder and suicide.

Very light or non-existent, skipped pressure of the pp*I* suggests a lack of some kind concerning the male or female image which it encompasses. This may mean that the writer feels that he has not really "known" or understood a parent, or it may suggest a reluctance on his

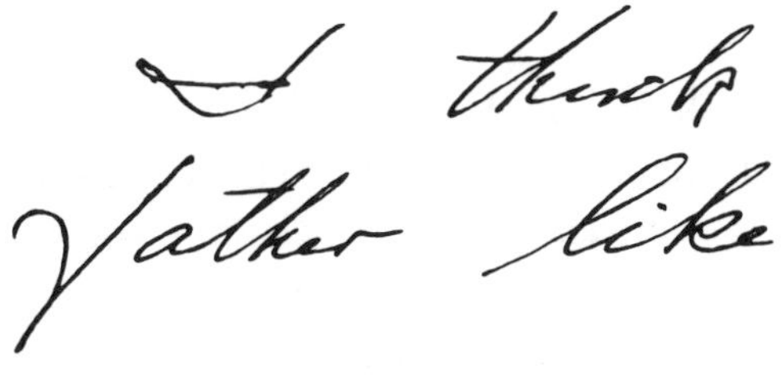

Fig. 136

part to become involved with a particular parent, male or female. Where the stroke is habitually so light that it skips or appears non-existent, the graphologist suspects serious emotional problems concerning the writer's reaction to the parental figure involved. The writing in Figure 136 is that of a 50-year-old woman who did not relate well to her mother. This fact has bothered her and sometimes caused difficulty in her relationships with others.

Fig. 137

Displaced pressure (upstroke heavy, downstroke light) indicates displacement of energies, as previously stated. Whe the pp*I* is consistently written in this fashion, difficulties in emotional control may be surmised. Displaced pressure in the ego symbols of children or adolescents may carry implications of self-doubt, possibly concerned with sexual identity. This hypothesis, however, still has to be borne out by research.

The writer of Figure 137 is a male, age 20. His relationship with his mother is poor. His mother continually kept the household in an uproar with her vascillating moods and tantrums. The retraced top of the *I* indicates tension and fear of criticism. The shaky ductus indicates need for reassurance. His reversed pp*I* is suggestive of a need for getting his own way.

The writer of Figure 138 is a female, age 28, with a strong relationship with her father. Her reversed pp*I* has a strongly pressured baseline horizontal stroke, displaced and showing feeling for the male figure. In this case, great

Fig. 138

emphasis is placed by the writer upon the help, both emotional and financial, which she received from her dad. She forms the father symbol first; the angular form echoes the father's harshness in general affairs. The writer has not found a man yet who measures up to her father.

Directional Pressure

Pressure from the right or left writing field changes a straight stroke into a curved one, or changes the form of a curved stroke. This is termed *directional pressure* and symbolizes influences on the writer from the symbolic field of the left or right areas of the writing, says graphologist Felix Klein.

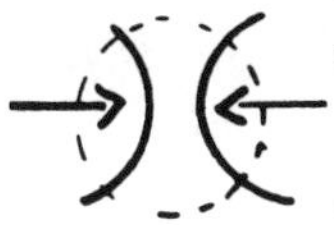

As previously indicated, the left is equated with *female,* the right with *male.* When the pp*I* is consistently bowed in one or the other direction, pressure influences are revealed.

Pressure from the symbolic *left* (field of the mother) indicates that relationships from the past are strong. There may be anxieties concerning mothering, or *female* events. Unresolved circumstances or problems may hamper the poise of the writer.

Pressure from the *right* (field of the father) pushes the pp*I* leftward—in other words, back. This stroke may manifest fear or concern about the future, and perhaps the father image. Anxiety over moving ahead negates the traditional "male" image.

Pressure From Left: The writer of Figure 139 is a female, age 17. Her relationship with her parents is poor.

I think - daughters

Fig. 139

She is troubled, feeling rejected and unworthy. A potentially good relationship with her mother has been cut off because of a divorce and remarriage. Note the directional pressure from the left. As she grew up, her father was unstable and a detriment to his family. She says she often considers suicide. There is no adequate female or male image within her pp*I*.

Pressure From Right: The writer of Figure 140 is a male, age 20. His relationship with his parents is poor. His

I am not going

Fig. 140

mother and father are both out of the picture so far as this young man is concerned. He left home at fifteen, did odd jobs and slept in doorways until he joined the Navy. He still has nightmares about the past and is a loner whose relationships with others are limited. He is most fearful, however, about the future and about his own male identification. Both difficulties are suggested by the caved-in form of his ego symbol.

The rest of the writing often indicates further expressions of directional pressure. For example, extensions of y, p, q, j, z, f or g will show caving-in from either side.

The upper directional pressure curves the top or bottom line of the printed *I* into a garland. This may imply influence of some kind from the upper zone. Whether such influence denotes negative or positive forces and what the value is for the writer depends largely upon other factors in the handwriting.

Lower directional pressure changes a straight horizontal line into a bowed curve, similar to an arcade. Some influence from the middle or lower zones is conveyed by this stroke on the printed *I*. Whether material, financial or bodily influences are at work cannot be ascertained without considering all the other elements of the handwriting.

The writer of Figure 141 is a male, age 58. His relationship with his mother is strong. The influence of a home dominated by the mother is shown in his pp*I*. The writer achieved no unifying identity with his father; communication died. Directional pressure is shown from

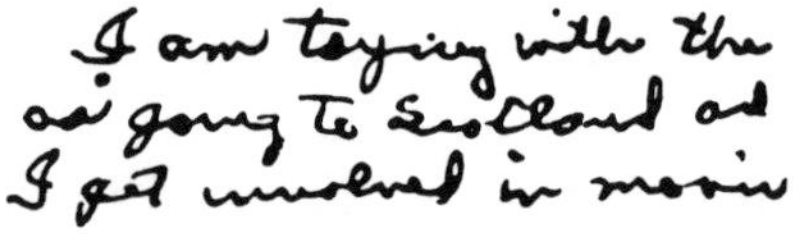

Fig. 141

the right in the upper zone, suggesting hampering ideas concerning the future. The writer expresses contempt for his father. He is not married and does not pursue typical masculine interests.

Chapter 7

SCOPE AS A MALE-FEMALE FACTOR

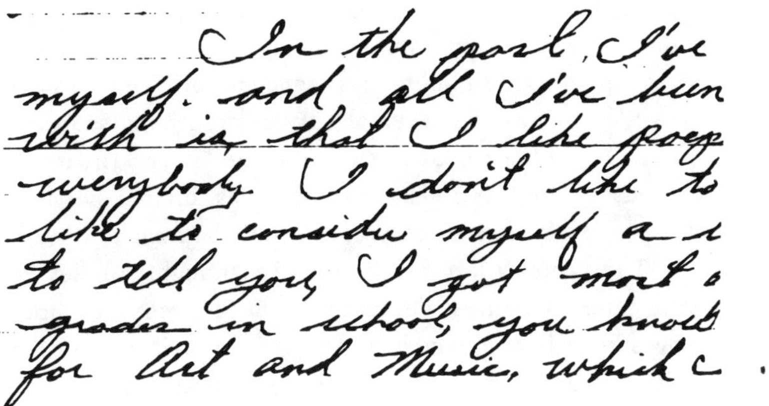

Fig. 142

Scope may be defined as the space needed for movement or activity, as well as the extent or range of operation. In applying this concept to the two parent figures within the ego symbol, we refer to space *within* the two figures, and to an extent the zones in which they are found.

The scope encompassed by the mother figure involves

193

a curved area: the female symbol is conventionally formed by a loop. A loop is unlike a circle in graphological terms. A circle may be either open or closed; a loop is so constructed that the final stroke crosses over the beginning stroke. The loop cannot be open except by a broken or incomplete stroke.

Loops form a frame or an enclosure which is a structure of the imagination. The scope of the loop within the ego symbol generally refers to the writer's imaginative concept regarding the female symbol. By limiting the breadth, or scope, of the loop—even to the point of pinched squeezing, retracing, or a single line—the writer limits his imagination and insight toward the female. By enlarging the scope of this loop, the writer may indicate unconsciously that he has broad, possibly far-flung interpretations of the female.

This application of imaginative thought applies to both parental figures within the pp*I*. The scope of both images reveals some inclinations of the writer to either limit or enlarge his concept or feelings concerning them.

Fig. 143

The retracing of the female symbol in Figure 143 suggests the writer's opposition to her mother. In this case, the writer's beloved father was divorced by the mother when the daughter was seven.

Fig. 144

The writer of Figure 144 is a male, age 23. His relationship with his parents is poor. His home life was disruptive, and he dislikes both his parents. The mother pampered and dominated him. His father was critical, sharp and disapproving. The writer has not been able to achieve a close relationship with women he admires. He does not permit close scrutiny of his motives and feels helpless when confronted with decisions. Note the desire to attain superiority over women: middle zone placement of the mother symbol and upper zone placement of the male symbol suggest displaced imagination. The angled father image and the yielding baseline stroke of the pp*l* suggest the writer is in a quandary: although he puts up a good front, he lacks self-confidence.

The loop which forms the mother figure begins normally on or slightly below the baseline. This placement of the beginning stroke is a graphic indicator of movement into the everyday, real world.

The beginning stroke, however, may start far below the baseline within the lower zone. Especially if this stroke is accompanied by displaced pressure, hostility or resentment concerning the female or mother figure may be suspected. The stroke emphasizes the propelling force driving the ego into action. Such display of fortified energy may be positive or negative, on behalf of the female or in opposition to her. Like other graphological symbols, inference must be drawn from all the factors within the handwriting.

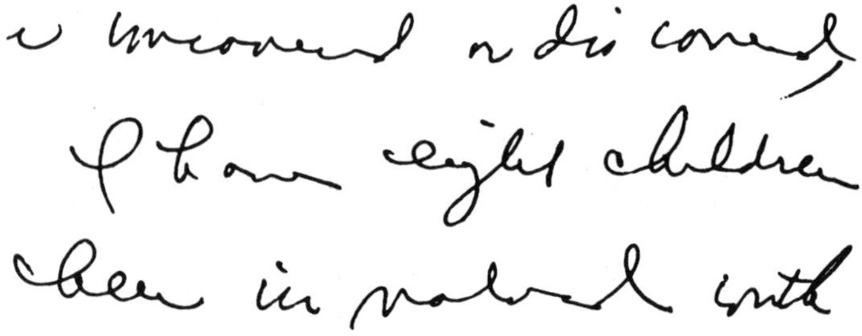

Fig. 145

The excessively slanted ego symbol in Figure 145 reflects the writer's hyper-reactions. The large scope and lower zone beginning stroke indicate her preoccupation with herself. The writer has an undisciplined imagination and is usually in a state of disorder. She cannot control her children, who are in trouble at home and in school. The total structure of her *I* has no balanced position on the baseline of the middle zone of reality. The writer is discouraged: she has a poor relationship with her husband and is overwhelmed by her responsibilities. She was raised without a father.

On the other hand, the female image loop may begin in the upper zone, above the baseline. Such a loop may be inflated or small, correlating in some instances with the writer's concepts concerning the female or the mother figure. The tiny loop or the loop which begins in the upper zone may imply both wishful thinking or fantasy concerning the female or the mother figure. Self-pity (if the writer is a female) and imaginative over-concern with the mother image may lie behind this tendency to escape the average middle zone placement of the symbol. Strong ambitions may also be associated with dilated loops.

Fig. 146

The writer of Figure 146 is a female, age 50. Her mother died when she was small. Her father later remarried and left her with her maternal grandparents. They kept alive the memory of their deceased daughter and were inclined to indulge their small grandchild. Note the imaginative female symbol as well as the incomplete male symbol suggesting her limited feelings toward her father.

The father figure is a combination of curve, angle and straight line: versatility of this image suggests in part the importance of the male within the home and outside it. Unusual emphasis on scope will often indicate strong feelings on the part of the writer concerning the image.

Squeezing the father symbol carries implications of questioning or consciously suppressing thoughts about his authority. Retracing implies the refusal to face facts. Limited scope implies limitation in value or effect of the male. This may, of course, result in either positive or negative results for the writer.

Zonal displacement of the male or female symbols in

the pp*I* usually suggests heightened reaction or response to the mother or father. It must be emphasized, however, that in creative handwriting of a high form level, zonal displacement may simply relate to the writer's imagination, energy and interests. What appears to be a negative diminution may simply offer evidence of a simplified approach to the ego symbol, even though independence from parents may also be implied.

In many instances, however, displacement indicates a need in the writer's emotional life. Such a need may sometimes be satisfied by surrogate figures such as a boyfriend or an older friend who can offer parental or maternal understanding.

Fig. 147

The writer of Figure 147 is a male, age 45. His identification with the father was poor. He did not enjoy a happy childhood. He was neglected by the father, who suffered from ill health and had little interest, time or energy for his family. The father at times seemed to be jealous of the son. The writer's wish for a satisfactory male identity is expressed through the displaced father symbol, hanging into the lower zone. His mother worked. She is displaced into the upper zone of imagination. The hard stroke of the male image is missing, and the ego symbol suggests pressure from the past. The father was hospitalized a great deal of the time when the writer was growing up and died when he was in his teens.

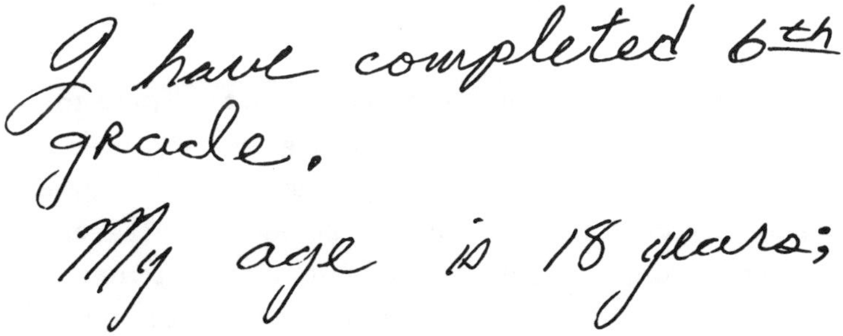

Fig. 148

The writing in Figure 148 reveals a need for both a mother and a father figure. The symbols are displaced in both the upper and the lower zone. The scope is large—this writer demands lots of elbow-room. Note that his ego symbol resembles a small *g*—the first initial of the writer's name. This may or may not be coincidental with the egocentricity suggested by its inflated size and scope. This is not the writing of an unintelligent person, but as in so many instances of emotional difficulty, the writer's schooling was interrupted.

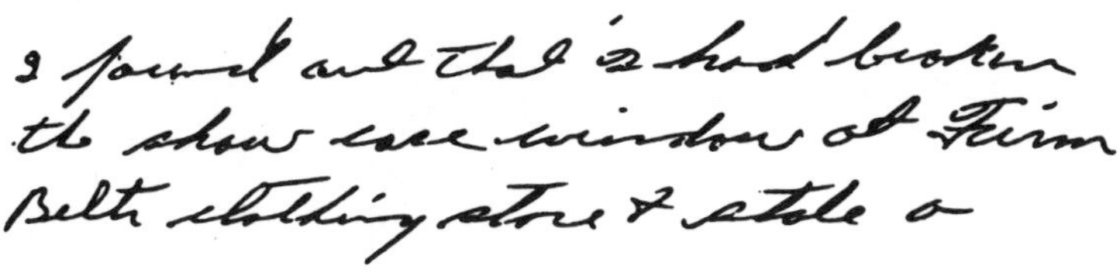

Fig. 149

The ego symbol of the writing in Figure 149 shows

distortion in all the male-female factors. The writer is serving a prison term and has received little treatment for his emotional problems. His self-concept is severely limited.

In summary, scope is related in some measure to the writer's feeling of security in dealing with the male and female authority figures. Constricted scope suggests limited growth in these areas of relationship; enlargement suggests some imagination or ambition concerning the writer's identification with parental and sexual symbols. Zonal placement of unusual or distorted figures indicates the focus of the writer's concern.

Chapter 8

ANGULARITY AS A MALE-FEMALE FACTOR

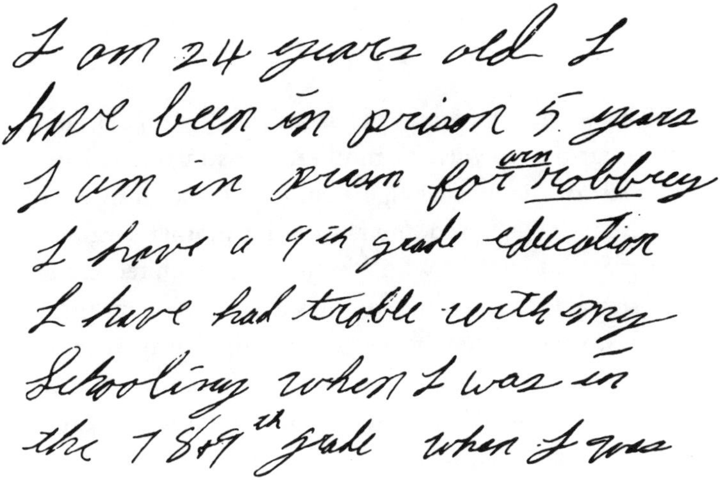

Fig. 150

The copybook *I* is written with only one angle. This is found in the male image as the final stroke turns from left to right.

The presence of angles not called for in the pp*I*

suggests an inflexible self-image. If such angles are found consistently in place of the soft loop or curve in the female image, chances are that this inflexibility is related to the writer's concept of the female image. The same connotation of inflexibility applies to angles found in the male symbol. It is more appropriate to find angles in the father figure. Strong angles or excessive size of angles, however, often suggest the writer's negative reactions even if the angles are in the correct place.

Fig. 151

The writer of Figure 151 is a male, age 27. He has a strong relationship with his mother. The straightened stoke on the left of the mother figure suggests his need to cut off from the past. The predominance of his mother's influence had a great deal to do with his choice of architecture as a profession. He is outgoing and has a good self-concept. He admits, however, that he needs to break away from the domination of his mother. He is about to move to another state, a change which appears to offer him the prospect of a more separate identity.

Fig. 152

A soft angle, shaped almost like a popsicle, instead of

the usual inverted curve, is sometimes found in the upper part of the mother figure. In some cases, this stroke seems to be related to the writer's feelings of mother protection. Actually the writer seems to "build a temple" for the figure in question. This may suggest some unusual aspect in his relationship with the mother figure, as is the case with the writer of Figure 152, who saw his mother murdered in a family quarrel.

Fig. 153

The father dominated the home of the writer who penned Figure 153. He was a patriarch from abroad and very autocratic. He believed that a woman's place is in the home; the writer is inclined to agree.

Angles are perhaps the most noticeable of the connections, especially when used in place of the conventional form. There are some general concepts which relate them to family harmony.

The first is the fact that angles are specific and distinct. Their starting-and-stopping movement slows up the fluidity of writing. The angle is written with a strict and definite contractive and expansive motion. To write in an angular fashion with grace and precision takes a great deal of effort, control and regularity, suggesting the writer's awareness of direction and method.

Second, angled writing of high quality implies intelligence, will-power and determination. In lower writing form, the angles tend to lose their grace and finesse, taking on qualities of hardness and rigidity. Inclination toward compulsive or prejudiced thinking may express itself in excessive angles. We may suspect lack of tact and/or authoritarianism if angles predominate in the handwriting.

Third, whatever the goals of the angle-writer may be, the concept of drive and tension lies behind them. Angles will imply a certain amount of aggression, overt or unexpressed. How productive or non-productive this aggression can be to the writer will depend in large measure upon the use to which it is put.

Fig. 154

The writer of Figure 154 is a male, age 28. His mother was the dominant figure in the household and told her son many times that his father did not understand him as well as she did. Her inflexibility and firmness of convictions are partly revealed through his angled female symbol. His father was a disappointment to him.

He is having some difficulty with his own marriage because he married a girl whom he hoped to dominate; however, she is a great deal like his mother. The rigid pp*I* suggests his tension.

An incompleted angle within the father-figure may suggest an incomplete concept of the male role, which as a rule is unsatisfactory to the writer. There may have been so little communication with the father that the writer has no real understanding of male parenting. Or the feelings toward the male figure may be particularly negative. Unusually angled strokes may suggest brutality, especially if accompanied by pressure.

Fig. 155a

The writer of Figure 155a is a male, age 18. His relationship with his parents is poor. His father regularly beats up the family members; his mother finds refuge in drinking. The writer has a long history of delinquency and, although bright, has not yet completed school. The extreme height of his pp*I* shows his need for supremacy. Aggressiveness is apparent in the male stroke, although it is incomplete. This boy never had a real father relationship.

Fig. 155b

Softness of stroke shown by a curve or loop in place of the angle normally gives evidence of a nebulous or ineffectual quality of the male parent figure. If the writer is male, lack of father-leadership is apt to affect the quality of his identification; if the writer is female, there may be a problem in relating satisfactorily to the father, and a resultant difficulty in establishing a satisfactory feminine-response pattern. The sample in Figure 155b was written by a woman who has had problems relating happily to her father and to other males.

Displacement and exaggeration of angularity appear to be negative signs within the pp*I* with respect to parental or male-female symbolism. Softness of the conventional angle contains negative or positive implications concerning the writer's identification with the male or female parent. Such factors affect the total gestalt of the self-image and offers a great many clues with respect to the writer's relationship with the opposite sex.

The printed *I* found in the cursive script not only suggests a need for independence, but may reflect feelings of closeness or separation from the parent figures or their counterparts. Closely connected parts of the angled Roman *I* maintain their psychological implications.

A lightly pressured, loosely formed top stroke which also has a consistent lack of meeting with the vertical stroke may show the writer's alienation from the female symbol.

A male image repeatedly disconnected from the center stroke may suggest the writer's removal from the father figure.

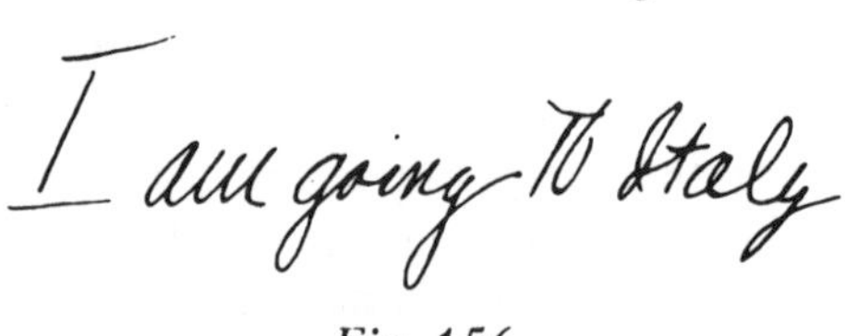

Fig. 156

The writer of Figure 156 grew up in a home where

few words were ever spoken even at mealtime. She is an only child and is essentially an independent but lonely person.

and I feel like us

Fig. 157a

The writings in Figures 157a and 157b belong to twin sisters who came to America from Germany when they were fifteen years old. Differences in their personality and temperament are shown by the differences in their writing. While the pp*I* forms are rather typically German, the one in Figure 157a is written by the twin who is the more aggressive, decisive and industrious. She is an excellent businesswoman. Note the angular slowness of the careful script. Always busy, she is a hard worker; exacting in her demands for others and herself.

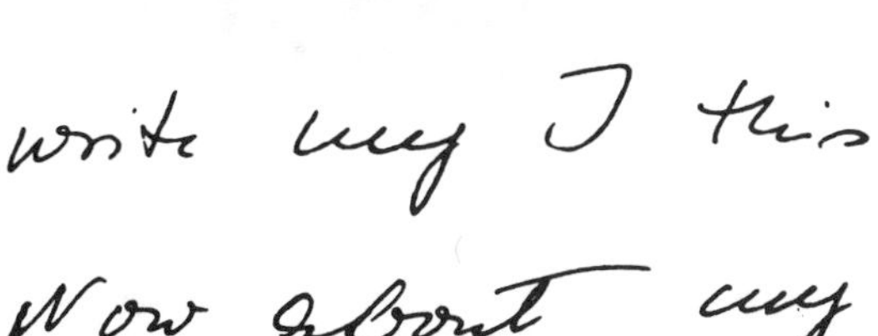

write my I this

Now about my

Fig. 157b

The writing of her twin sister in Figure 157b reflects her spontaneous and easy-going nature. It is fluently garland with much fast threading. She is impulsive and finds her place by being pleasant and charming. As a child she was sickly and received a great deal of attention from her parents. Her sister received attention by being efficient and capable. Aspects of their life styles are closely echoed by their written ego symbols. The pp*I* in Figure 157b is more yielding than the angular pp*I*'s in Figure 157a, although both sisters were taught the German letter.

Chapter 9

ELABORATION AS A MALE-FEMALE FACTOR

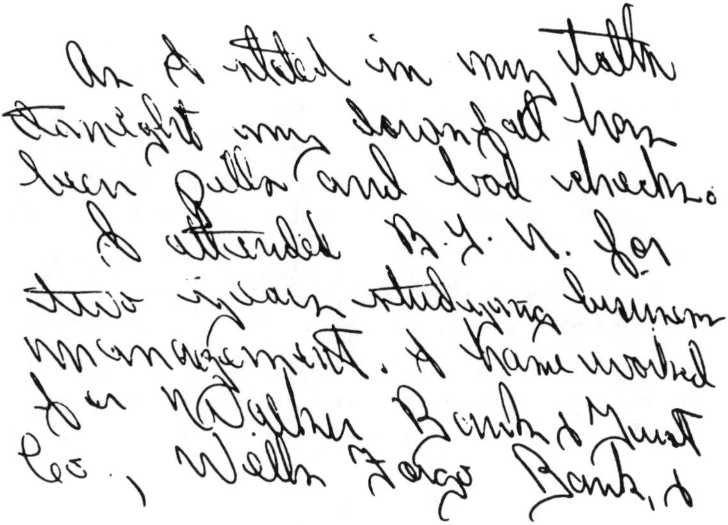

Fig. 158

Whenever a male or female image within the pp*I* shows exaggeration, the analyst is alerted to the possibility that the writer may be particularly sensitive.

Elaboration or embellishment of handwriting is usually done in order to impress or convince the writer, as well as others, that things are better than they really are. It is generally true that the more a writer elaborates his personal pronoun, the less insight he possesses about himself.

Interest in being considered creative may be suspected if the writer manipulates additional flourishes within the pp*I*. However, since many creative handwritings involve simplified motion, actual creativity is not necessarily evidenced by elaborated writing, although it may be. The simplification of the creative writing suggests independence from parental and other influences, with commitment primarily to self-actualization.

Elaboration sometimes suggests that the writer is prone to waste his time, occupying himself with unnecessary details. Often a real or imagined deficiency bothers such a writer. Use of loops or circles implies some worry or preoccupation, with probable solution of tension through imagination or fantasy.

Spiraling loops in or around the mother-figure are often accompanied by a weak male symbol; the opposite may be true if the exaggeration is within the father image.

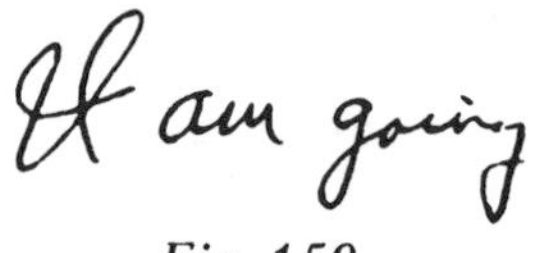

Fig. 159

The pp*I* in Figure 159 is reversed: the writer wants to have his own way. The large size of the father symbol emphasizes the writer's desire to be his own man. The mother symbol is, nevertheless, larger than the male symbol; the mother dominated the household. The area of maleness is a sensitive one psychologically for this writer. Note that he elaborates and writes the male image ahead of the female one.

The act of imagining or forming a particular mental concept regarding the male image is sometimes indicated by the addition of a loop on the stroke before terminating it. Particularly if pressure, size, slant and other factors are also emphasized within that area, the concept of the male figure may be distressing to the writer.

Fig. 160

The writer of Figure 160 is a male, age 20. He has a strong relationship with his mother. He never knew his real father and grew up in a home with a stepfather whom he resented. He was close to his mother who provided a stable home life in spite of her husband's gambling habit. He has not been a problem in school but is having difficulty at present deciding what to do with his life; he is drifting. The reversed pp*I* and the imagination loop in the father symbol point to dissension. The garland base is yielding, not firm; no strong father-leadership is evident.

A pp*I* with added loops may suggest particular attitudes centered around either the male or female symbol, depending on which figure the loops embellish. By elaborating his pp*I* in this fashion, the writer may be symbolizing some aspects of his relationship with his parents that shaped his reaction to the idea of male or female.

Fig. 161

The writer of Figure 161 is a woman, age 38. Although she grew up in a conventionally oriented home, and relationships are at present harmonious in her own married life, she is sensitive to the problem of drinking, which her father possessed. The additional loop within the male figure appears to express her disappointment in men.

Fig. 162

The writer of Figure 162 is a young woman, age 19. She has been involved with drugs for several years. She was outwardly conforming until her father died when she was fourteen. After that she was a rebel in the home, which the mother had dominated. She always used to side with the father in family quarrels and had been his favorite of four children. She loved her father and the loop within the male image in her pp*I* suggests her special feelings toward him. She is sensually inclined and says she needs the good feelings which drugs give her; her pasty writing evidences her sensitiveness to such physical stimuli.

The accented image which sometimes results in the

Fig. 163

pp*I* resembling a butterfly or a number may indicate a writer who feels he must go to himself for the answers. This kind of writer has often developed an acute case of independence which may prove a hindrance to him in relating intimately to other people. The overly-arcaded stroke suggests a shielding of the emotions. Male and/or female areas may be written as in Figure 163.

Fig. 164

The writer of Figure 164 loved her father and felt protective of him. He was a very unaggressive person who usually retreated from all the commotion created by his large family. The writer herself is sociable but requires quite a bit of privacy.

Elaboration of the pp*I* may be accomplished in part by retracing the top of the female or male symbol: such retracings imply repression on the part of the writer. The writer may be able to "forget" facts which are painful to him. This unconscious eliminating process is, paradoxically enough, expressed through elaboration. Symbolically, the writer is narrowing rather than enlarging. His sensitivity to criticism from parental figures may be marked.

Fig. 165

Elaboration of the female image in Figure 165 appears correlated with the writer's occupation as a dress designer. She enjoys decorating the human form and enjoys her role as a woman. She runs her household very well and is an excellent hostess.

Fig. 166

The writing in Figure 166 is that of a young woman, age 27 whose weak and ineffectual father caused her discouragement and heartache as she grew up. He was an alcoholic artist who had a difficult time supporting and maintaining a family. The tiny structure and downward terminal suggest her discouragement with the male sex. She has trouble relating well to men.

Fig. 167

Although she loved and wanted to be with her father, the writer in Figure 167 was raised by relatives after her mother died. (Note the beginning stroke of the female stroke in the upper zone of imagination.) The formation of the male symbol in the lower zone suggests her great concern over her relationship with her father, emphasized by pressure and a final hook to the left. She is a friendly but reserved person.

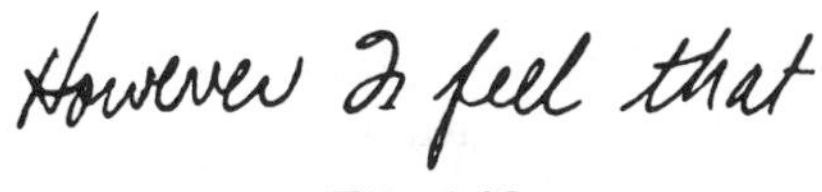

However I feel that

Fig. 168

The sample in Figure 168 is that of a man whose home revolved around the father. He was an executive who was gone from the household much of the week, but he dominated the family over the weekends. His mother played a less important role to her son than his father did. The parents were temperamentally different with different interests. This writer wishes to be identified as a strong person. Note the added brace stroke at the end of the pp*I*..

A need for emotional support concerning the self-image may characterize the writer who elaborates the scope of his ego-symbol, particularly if such elaboration involves the protective distance which circles may give. Such enclosures appear to represent some need of an encompassing mother or female figure. Dependence upon superstition or magic may help such a writer cope with a limited sense of himself.

The pp*I* with a circle around it, the humped,

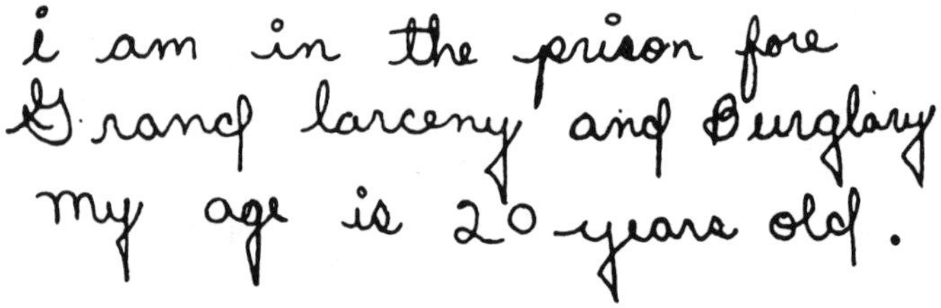

Fig. 169

foetal-like *I,* or the small, looped baby *i* shown in Figure 169, all suggest to the trained graphologist that justification of the self is difficult to attain.

PART III

THE EVOLVING SELF

Chapter 1

CHILD: TALLY–AND OTHERS

Childhood is where "all that is to be" begins. The poet has put it succinctly: "The child is father to the man."

What then about children's handwriting? Does the child's *I* and signature have special significance?

Although norms for graphological evaluation of children's handwriting have not been established, the uniqueness of each child is generally reflected in his handwriting. In spite of stereotyped teaching, the writing reflects his distinctive personality. And to the trained eye, the pp*I* and the signature appear to be particularly sensitive to reflections of the self.

Handwriting is *written* behavior. Even with children one can equate superior writing with even pressure, consistent speed and size, simplicity and good use of paper space. Inconsistencies, however, do not necessarily reflect emotional or physical problems, since actual physiological development and maturity may vary considerably, even in a few months' period. Nor can we compare Johnny with Susie, although they may be in the same grade.

Poor perceptual ability of the child, for instance, may not reflect mental retardation no matter how "bad" or messy the writing appears. Lack of manual dexterity in writing at the age of ten does not necessarily mean that the small writer lacks emotional control. The child may simply lag in this one area. No matter how poor we may consider the writing to be, even retarded children may give some evidence of their individuality through their attempts at scribbling. The following samples from a camp for retarded children offer clues to the writers' differing personalities. Each child is around eight years of age.

Fig. 170

The girl who wrote Figure 170 is very withdrawn. Note the left-tending motion. She hides and refuses to see visitors much of the time. She is dreamy and inclined to sulk. The loops and flaccid garlands reflect her imagination and lack of initiative.

The writer of Figure 171 is argumentative and defiant. No matter how much attention he receives, it is never enough. His tendencies toward hostile acting-out and "delinquent" behavior are expressed through his dark,

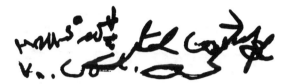

Fig. 171

filled-in periods and blotchy writing.

The sharp peaks on the "signature" of the retarded girl who wrote Figure 172 indicate her willingness

Fig. 172

to learn; the large size suggests her need for attention. She was always first at the door when visitors came and has a persistent curiosity.

In contrast to the scribblings of these mentally handicapped children, let us introduce you to Tally, a "normal" eight-year-old, who is in danger of failing third grade. Whatever work Tally does perform is "100 per cent," but often he chooses not to perform. His teacher says: "If he cannot be motivated to do *all* his work, he will not be promoted."

The two detailed analyses of Tally's handwriting which follow illustrate how revealing a normal child's

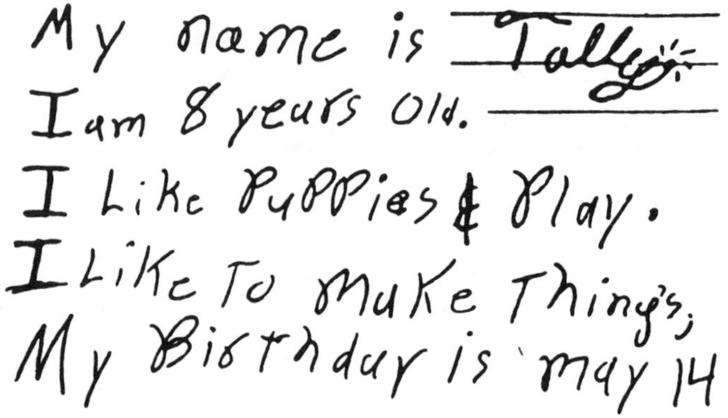

Fig. 173

handwriting can be of his personality.

The first report, by Leslie W. King, utilized outside resources as well as Tally's handwriting. These are enumerated preceding her graphological report.[1]

A Graphological Report
—by Leslie W. King

Preparatory work for a study of Tally's problems: To prepare the analysis of the writing of this eight-year-old, a request was made for a sample of the school model, provided by the teacher. A sample of his duplication of her printing, prepared in school, was submitted. Additionally obtained, was a sample prepared with ball point pen on unlined paper with three carbon copies. He was also requested to do the Draw-A-Person Test and to make a

---

1. The following reports were both published in the *Newsletter of the American Association of Handwriting Analysts,* January and February, 1971.

kinetic family relationships drawing. Finally, a sample of each of his parent's writing was required, as well as his siblings'.

Before the written report was submitted, discussion was held with the parents, using a frequency distribution graph and a Table as a foundation for a well-rounded, comprehensive understanding of their son's problems in school and their several causes. Such a discussion always stimulates the parents to relate specific incidents to the traits being explained and assures insight and deeper understanding when they read the report later.

Summary of the graphological report: Tally's range of degrees of strength of 40 evaluated personality traits was from .50-6.0, on a scale with a possible high of 10.0 and a median of 3.0-5.0. His strongest traits are self-esteem; involvement with people and causes; ego needs; expedient personality; well eveloped emotional and social factors, though on a superficial level; inventiveness and originality; anti-social personality patterns; self-motivation; inhibitions and feelings of inferiority. Significant low-scoring traits are: conformity, physical energy, insight, self-control, functional productivity.

The four and one-half page report discusses relationships in the family that directly affect Tally. It includes reference to his unfulfilled needs where his parents are concerned. It explains how a few of their normal behavior patterns and attitudes are actually detrimental to their son in his present stage of personality development.

The parental attitudes of perfectionism—verging on compulsiveness; the father's impatience and the mother's customary habit of continuing with her work while listening to her son, all undermine his self-confidence and threaten his ego. Other parental behavior patterns were discussed and suggestions made to help them build their son's self-confidence and to overcome his subconscious need to protect his ego by any means expedient at the time of threat—real or imagined.

This is the writing of a boy who has a much higher than average intelligence for his age level. He has genuine creative talent that should be carefully retained. He is independent; self-starting; is motivated to work towards perfection and to avoid at all cost what he fears he will perform inadequately or imperfectly at. He can be very persevering about what he wants—or does not want. He is observant; meticulous; and will willingly strive to meet his own ideal—even if it beyond his present capability.

He does not passively conform to other people's standards and can't be motivated through a system of rewards and punishments based on the idea of "fitting in." His absorption with perfectionism is a result of conditioning through the parental attitudes.

What is important to Tally and what causes him to do some of his schoolwork and to (seemingly) stubbornly refuse to do the rest? Importance is based on whether a project stimulates him and whether or not he feels he can tackle it 100% successfully and whether or not it affords him ego satisfaction through doing it. Fear, insecurity, feelings of inadequacy and self-doubt are behind his refusal to undertake some schoolwork. Excessive, step-by-step encouragement by his mother, which she has done in the past, is to be avoided. His father is his ego-ideal. Motivational rewards based on increased father-son relationships will stimulate this child.

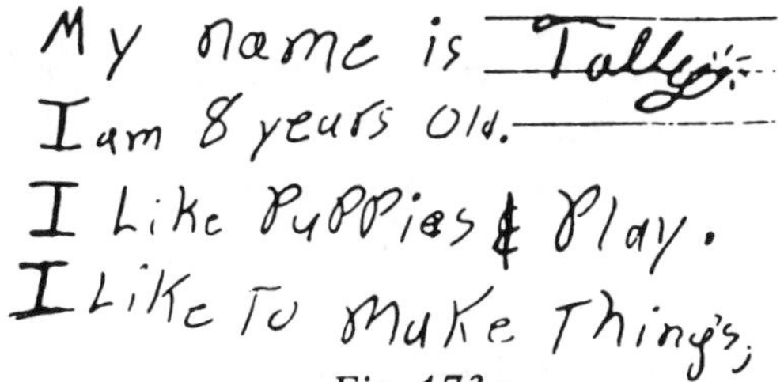

My name is _Tally_
I am 8 years Old._____
I Like Puppies & Play.
I Like To Make Things;

Fig. 173a

A Graphological Report
—by Jane N. Green

Analysis of Tally's signature and personal pronoun I:
The *I* of Tally, as well as his signature, convey a great deal about his school problem, for it is essentially one of ego-involvement which he finds overwhelming.

The noticeably heavy writing of the signature is matched by his heavily pressured, retraced pp*I*. Retracing and heaviness is emphasized in all three structures of the ego symbol, yet not in the rest of the writing. Such pressure and overlay indicate secretiveness, anxiety and tension about the self which are in part allayed through extra emphasis when he symbolizes himself in writing.

That the writer is fully aware of his importance is sugested by his tall printed pp*I*. He is a self-conscious child who, nevertheless, has a feeling of real independence and self-esteem. He wants to do things his own way, and do them perfectly. There is strength as well as weakness in such angular retracings. Perfectionistic tendencies cause emotional stress to this small writer, denoted by the preoccupation with his pp*I* before proceeding to the rest of the sentence.

His signature denotes equal sensitiveness, although it is not as heavily emphasized as the *I*. He is just learning to write in a cursive fashion and his control is not good. Nevertheless, he is surprisingly fluid in these writing movements and proceeds with flair to the end. He bears down as he writes his name; excessive emotionality and hostility are implied by the filled-in final. But notice the star-like blaze he dashes around this small darkness: Tally finishes his signature with a sparkler! Ambivalent feelings and a certain amount of despair are emphasized by this action, coupled with the conviction that what the writer does has considerable merit; he will go on his own way nevertheless.

The creativity of this child is signified by his non-copybook approach, particularly in the signature. Inventiveness and originality are essential ingredients in his personality. The graphologist would suspect that Tally will simplify his writing further as he develops and matures; he appears to be creative.

Handicapped and oppressed by school demands which he considers trivial, the writer might do better in a school which allows freedom of both mental and physical movement: the well-run modular system, an "open" or "free" school, or a good private school would meet, theoretically, the needs of this dynamic but inhibited youngster. Less regimentation would be appealing to a youngster of this calibre. Essentially, it appears to be his imagination which is hindering school progress: his strong traits will be reinforced by less attention to rules and more attention to his individuality and personal sense of integrity. Strong angular emphasis of the ppl suggests that this child values aggressiveness, as well as lack of conformity.

Chapter 2

ADOLESCENT: GLORIA—AND OTHERS

Adolescence has been described as the higher court of appeals—where the decisions of the lower court of childhood have a last good chance of being reversed. Adolescence is a period in which the direction of development can be set toward normalcy rather than toward neuroticism or psychosis.

The hope is that this "higher court" will not merely reaffirm the decisions of the lower: i.e., the child was a failure; therefore, the adolescent will also be a failure. The hope is that adolescent experiences may temper and alleviate bad beginnings. Graphological techniques can aid counselors in spotting deep-seated conflicts whose resolution is essential before the next developmental step can be taken.

The writing in Figure 174 belongs to Gloria, a young fifteen-year-old girl, a potential dropout from high school.

Gloria has lived all her life in an impoverished neighborhood and was, at the time of this writing,

229

participating in a Work Experience Program with a part-time school schedule and a part-time work program

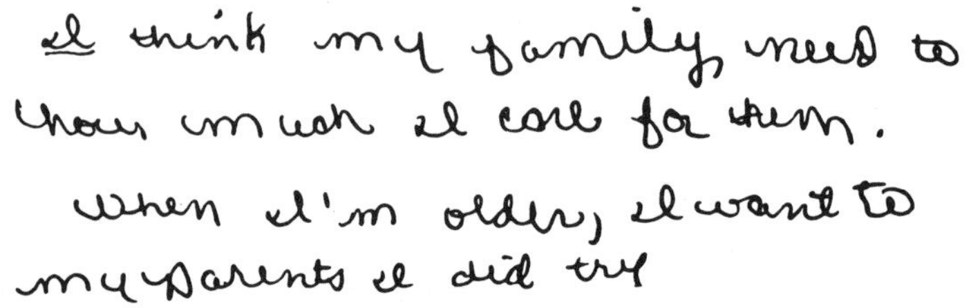

I think my family need to know how much I care for them.

When I'm older, I want to my parents I did try

Fig. 174

for which she was paid. This funded program is an effort to help able children to rise above their environmental problems. Gloria was employed part time as a clerk in a large firm.

The following two evaluations—one by the counselor and coordinator of the program and the other by the author—were made independently of each other.

The author based her evaluation on a study of Gloria's written *I*'s in their relation to words around them and to the writing page. The several pages of writing which were used included about thirty personal pronouns. It was a blind analysis: the subject and analyst had not met. The coordinator-counselor obtained his data through testing devices such as the Coopersmith Self-Esteem Inventory, Stanford-Binet Intelligence Test, Iowa Achievement Tests and cumulative school data, as well as personal interviews and observations.

Coordinator-Counselor's Report

This student is in the lower 10% of the ninth grade class, maintaining a straight D average since seventh grade. She measured in the seventh percentile on the Gates MacIntyre Reading Test given in the school system.

A. *Self-concept: fluctuating.*

B. *Motivation: Conflict in will; she has little consistent drive.*

C. *Personality assets: Capability in practical things.*

D. *Expressed worries, fears: Conceals most of her feelings but is defensive and self-protective, as well as acting out aggression.*

E. *Behavioral observations: Varying conformity and bluntness.*

F. *Adjustment to authority: Hostility.*

G. *Future Aspirations: She has none; lives in the here and now. Feels only the present is of importance at this time.*

The girl is in ninth grade. Her I.Q. is 100. She wears the latest style clothes, flamboyant and colorful. However, the feminine effect is lessened because she walks and talks like a boy. In the school, she uses a lot of profanity, usually to create an image of self-importance. She is a leader among certain girls.

She has three brothers. Her family history includes the usual socio-economic problems common in a lower-class disadvantaged family from the inner-city ghetto. Her parents are divorced; mother works part-time. There is no evidence of a tight-knit family unit; the father appears frequently to steal from the family and beat up the children whether they need it or not. The mother's lack of interest in the children and the father's absence contribute to a disintegrated family life.

The girl completely despises her father because of his ill-treatment of the family. This attitude carries over in her feelings of distrust and hatred for men in general. She has a slightly better relationship with her mother, possibly only because she is also female. The girl resents her mother because of lack of interest in the home and family. The girl keeps the house very clean because she dislikes clutter and dirt.

The girl feels her parents hate each other, with no expectations or ambitions for either her or her brothers. This lack of expectation has made her somewhat a discipline problem.

Contradictory behavior indicates her inner uncertainty. At times she appears confident; at other times moody, depressed and overly sensitive to criticism. She is above average in her moving about from neighborhood to neighborhood; she has attended only three schools totally. Her attendance record has been extremely poor since the sixth grade. However, since she has been on the work program, she has not missed one day of work or one day of school—a real accomplishment.

Graphological Report

A. *Identification with mother: Ambivalent; average to poor.*
B. *Relationship to father: Poor.*
C. *Authority figure in the home: Mother.*
D. *Relationship of parents to each other: Not unified.*

The writer fluctuates in her feelings concerning herself. Her self-esteem varies according to her feelings of security within a group. Such fluctuations are undoubtedly based on anxiety. We would expect her to be depressed, moody and unpredictable at times. She has mixed emotions concerning herself as a female, although she relates far better to women than to men. She views men as dangerous and troublesome and has feelings of hostility and disappointment so far as they are concerned. She resents much about her environment and will present a discipline problem when things don't suit her. However, she wishes things to improve for her and if encouraged will respond positively.

Looking at her pp*I*, we find the above-mentioned factors clearly indicated. First, note the fluctuations in the height and width of the mother symbol. Such fluctuation indicates ambivalence toward the mother or any female surrogate, as well as toward the writer's role in life as a woman. Nevertheless, we see the female symbol is firmly braced on the writing baseline of reality, and thus we surmise that she operates, or has the potential to operate, in a practical, realistic manner. She may enjoy dealing with tangible things pertaining to being a female, such as household affairs, and clothes. Interest and appreciation of color, form and texture are indicated by the pastose line of writing. There is less tension in the mother symbol than in the father symbol as written.

The father symbol is written in deviating form, indicating some stress or disappointment concerning the male. Note the loop—the writer wishes things were different with her father. The sharpness of the stroke when the loop closes shows extreme hostility toward the father and perhaps males generally. Extra-heavy pressure on the male symbol indicates strong feelings concerning males and we suggest that she is affected deeply by them. She may well be in competition with them.

The writer does not view the parents as unified or integrated in a harmonious fashion. Note the separation between the two symbols. The mother is probably the authority figure within the home, so far as the writer is concerned, since the female symbol is more consistently written and more in the copybook manner than the male symbol.

The size of the pp*I* varies from tall to tiny in relation to the rest of her writing. We therefore realize the writer fluctuates in her feelings of adequacy. She probably acts quite differently with different persons, since her writing is predominantly garland and flexible. Such fluctuations are undoubtedly anxiety-provoking.

The backhand slant of writing emphasizes her defensiveness and watchfulness concerning what happens to her. The pp*I* is written backwards, beginning with the father symbol, ending to the right with the mother symbol. We thereby realize that the writer disliked authority as she grew up and probably is still fighting her environment. She is very capable of dissension and opposition.

Three Adolescents

In contrast to the self-image of Gloria, let us look at three other handwritings of young people. John's writing is shown in Figure 174. He is sixteen years old and a good

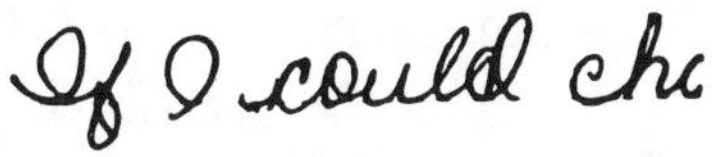

Fig. 174

student in junior high. John is conforming and successful in his superficial school relationships. However, his masculine sense of self is limited. There is virtually no real male image within his written ego symbol. He is not sure of his male identity and feels a great need to keep his guard up, as his arcade *I* suggests. Although friendly, he lacks a girl friend and finds it equally difficult to make boy friends with whom he feels at ease. John's garland writing is quite feminine in quality. His father is a successful businessman who is gone a great deal of the time. Most of the upbringing of his son has been left to the wife.

Figure 175 is the writing of Susan, a young girl who is

I'm depressed

Fig. 175

also sixteen. She is artistic as well as socially inclined. Her need to be popular has caused her to go around with anyone who could accept her; she has little self-confidence, as her inflated (need for attention) but squashed ego symbol indicates. Tremulous, weak pressure on the masculine image suggests the writer's difficulties with males; Susan views herself largely as a sex object.

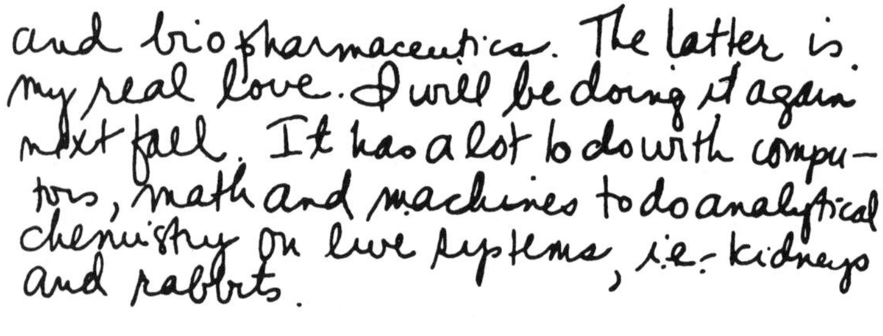

and biopharmaceutics. The latter is my real love. I will be doing it again next fall. It has a lot to do with computors, math and machines to do analytical chemistry on live systems, i.e.- kidneys and rabbits.

Fig. 176

The writing in Figure 176 is in great contrast to that of Gloria and the other three handwritings. It belongs to a nineteen-year-old university student, a girl who has a firm sense of self. She is capable, ambitious and enthusiastic about what she does. Note the firmly consistent pressure, the simplified letter forms and good rhythm within the total script.

Her pp*I* contains well balanced forms of both male and female images: although the writer is an only child, she was raised by discerning parents who taught their daughter to become independent. The ego symbol is of modest, unassuming size, is upright (she thinks before she acts) and emphasizes all three writing zones in good balance. The total form level is excellent, reflecting the writer's qualities of good judgment, involvement with other people, and dynamic goal-direction.

Chapter 3

ADULT: BETTE MAE

The transition from young adulthood to mature adulthood can be as stormy and difficult as adolescence. So says Menninger Foundation psychiatrist Dr. Herbert Lemme, who has been formulating concepts of adult development. The "mid-life crisis" may require major adjustments to the world of work, to the sense of personal achievement or lack of it, or to disruptive tragedies such as divorce or death.

Because we operate in accordance with our self-image, the written pp*I* reflects growing maturity and changes in character and personality. A new way of forming the ego symbol and signature often occurs after a change in life circumstances which affects the writer's self-concept.

The two handwritings in Figures 177 and 178 were written by the same woman in two distinct periods of her life. Figure 177 was penned a few years before the sudden

239

death of her husband. Figure 178 was written a year following his death.

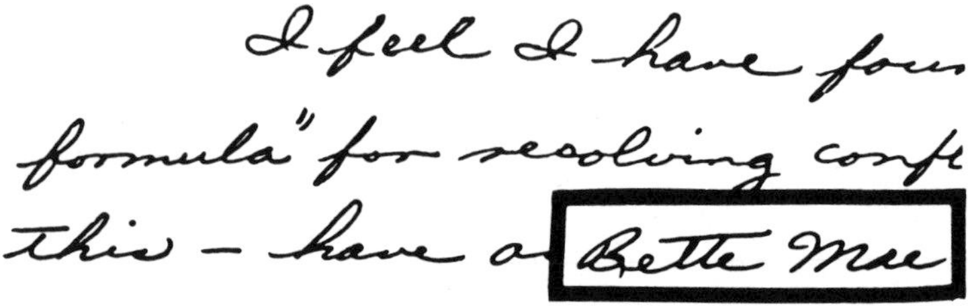

Fig. 177

Bette Mae is in her mid-forties. Her marriage was extremely harmonious and fulfilling; she enjoyed her role as a wife and as a mother to three very successful sons. Her self-image during her marriage was that of a conventional homemaker who was active in the community and enjoyed domesticity. Note the flexible, outgoing writing motion and conforming pattern of the signature and personal pronoun. Note, too, that her ego symbol emphasizes, through pressure, the male image more than the female: Bette Mae was strongly influenced by her beloved grandfather. A sensitive person, she married the right man and adapted easily to marriage, thoroughly enjoying her all-male household.

This early writing is generally light in pressure. The upward slant of the baseline echoes the writer's enthusiasm for life. Garland terminals and the outreaching final *I*-stroke suggest the writer's interest in others. The signature and the personal pronouns are in harmoniously moderate, conventional form.

After her husband's death, Bette Mae faced a

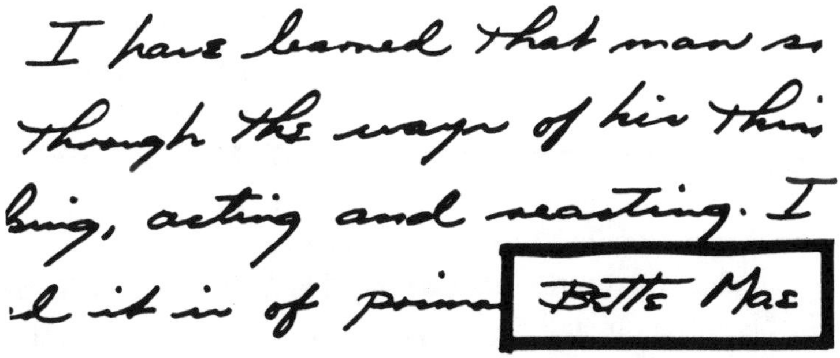

Fig. 178

re-evaluation of her life-style. Her personality, still outgoing, fun-loving and forward-looking, had to find new avenues of expression. Both her writing generally and her ppI and signature reflect changes in her self-image.

The ego symbol is now larger, printed and heavily pressured: these factors indicate the writer's independent thinking. Bette Mae no longer fits the role of a yielding, conforming housewife. The angular structure tells us that she views herself now as a separate entity who must be concerned with ideas, goals and practical considerations. Previously content to follow her husband's lead, she must now think for herself.

She is not living in a dream-world; rather, she has progressed to a simple, uncluttered view of herself as an individual who stands more or less alone. At this point in her life, the writer is self-concerned; note that the female image is longer than the male image in her printed ppI's. This is a reversal from the previously male-dominated conventional ppI she used to write.

Bette Mae's signature has also changed. The first two

given names are printed in a fashion to the Roman numeral
I and reflect an outer self-concept harmonious with her
private view. The given names are separated more fully
from the married last name and are more angular in
formation. Individuality and thinking qualities are
emphasized in both the pp*I* and signature.

The rest of the handwriting likewise indicates Bette
Mae's different and new approach to the world. Now she
feels the need to hold others more at a distance, for an
attractive widow is in a more vulnerable position than a
married woman. She does not wish to present an
unchecked, free-and-easy target. A symbol of this buffer
against the world is the Greek ϵ with which she terminates
many words: graphologically, these are classic examples of
cultural, intellectual or aesthetic interests. This arcade
stroke is a cover-up and checking motion which lessens the
outreaching, rightward movement of writing. It symbolizes
in part the curtailment of Bette Mae's enthusiastic nature,
as well as her interest in things at present beyond the
ordinary. Always philosophical, Bette Mae now emphasizes
more than ever the intellect. In spite of an outgoing
personality, a certain caution accompanies her actions.

The heavily pressured script suggests strong emotional
recall of the past. The simplified lower zone also reflects
new concepts about herself: at the present time she is not
interested in material possessions or in sexual expression.
She is emphasizing good judgment and freedom from
material and physical considerations, indicated by the
straight, unlooped lower extensions of letters.

As a person matures emotionally and mentally, he is

able, in general, to deal with reality without fantasizing. It appears that Bette Mae is adapting successfully to her new condition, as we all must, if we are to make the painful transition from one developmental level to another and, despite our fears and anxieties, move forward toward self-evolving growth.

Chapter 4

THE CONSISTENCY OF CHANGE

The graphological exploration of our intriguing *I*-land has been a dual adventure—an interior journey into the self, and an exterior journey into the .environment of the self.

The inner self is multiple, yet unified and evolving; the outer climate, too, is ever-changing. We strive for balance between being ourselves and cooperating with the social and historic change around us. Gordon Allport, the noted psychologist, has said that "handwriting is simply one example of the compromise we all reach between cultural obedience and individual integrity."

As was stated in an earlier chapter, to say that a person is inconsistent is paradoxical: in spite of apparent change, a person is consistently himself. The evolution of Bette Mae's handwriting and personality illustrates graphically the truth that inconsistency is always in terms of the observer, not the doer. Change, for her, simply underscored fidelity to the evolving self as it adjusted to an altered environment.

245

The unity of spirit within any historic age is reflected by its creative art forms: music, drama, as well as everyday accessories of home and fashion, architecture and design, come to us as visual echoes of the society from which they developed. This reflection of society appears to be generally true of handwriting forms which are taught as school models.

We cannot excape the conclusion that, like other patterns, school-model or copybook writing patterns are intrinsic forms of history, reflecting some of the mental, emotional, social and physical tendencies of the times. The fancy, ornate Spencerian script echoes a fussy Victorian era; the discipline of the early push-pull Palmer writing exercises were hallmarks of a vigorous American era. Just as a person's handwriting is compatible with his emotional spirit, popular writing forms appear compatible with the society around it. Copybook models, like art forms, may be termed abstractions from life itself.

A fundamental revision of attitude toward marriage and the male and female relationship is currently a vital new direction in our evolving society. Women's Liberation Movement and the growing independence of male and female today allow each to do his or her "own thing." Women's role is changing—the role of men, also, is in a state of flux. Campus unrest expressed the dawning of an age which prizes freedom and individuality.

Such changes may be expected to become part of accepted culture. Already, alterations within the social and sexual male-female structures are reflected all the way from university coed dormitories to elementary schools.

We are not surprised, therefore, to discover significant changes within the current commonly taught copybook writing models. We may now ask, have these societal shiftings affected the capital *I* as it is taught in the lower grades?

The first cursive writing is begun generally during the third grade, when the child is eight years old. Significantly, within the past eight years, the revision of cursive letter formations taught as standard in a number of school districts reflects new male-female concepts which appear relevant to our changing teenage society. In evaluating the "proper letter formations" taught in many elementary schools, the graphologist is struck by changes in the relationship between the male and female symbols of the capital *I*: each symbol is now separate, with no union or sphere of integration, which was common for several generations within the older copybook models.

Not only is the placement relationship altered, but the formation of the male symbol itself (in contrast with the more dominant female symbol) is lessened. The masculine image is softer, more left-tending, less future-oriented, more totally regressive. The angularity, expressive of a going-out toward others and actively indicated in the older Palmer or Zaner-Bloser modified capitals, is missing. Although the originators of the new school models are not consciously aware of what they are doing, the changing capital *I* reflects the social changes around them.

Many writers of the new personal pronoun *I*'s appear to have less interest and involvement in business and social affairs; withdrawal from competition in favor of nature orientation are stressed by both sexes. Women are demanding rights unheard of a generation ago. Men are being challenged on all fronts. Whether indicated by "copping out" or by revolutionary bomb-throwing, the fact is that in our western culture today, neither male nor female role has remained static. Neither has the expression of handwriting school models, symbolizing, as they do, the self-image.

What has weakened the traditional male self-concept? Many educators today are deeply concerned about the "feminization" of the American boy. Only fairly recently have behavioral scientists and teachers pointed out the damage done through emphasis on test-passing, "good" behavior and conformity to the mold. Male norms such as courage, inner direction, adventure-seeking, and a certain toughness in mind and body have not been emphasized in the average school learning situation. Women, by and large, have monopolized and set the standards for behavioral norms in the schools. Competitive grading, pigeon-holing of youngsters' abilities and establishing set rules of school conduct have damaged the self-esteem of many youngsters who could not make "grades."

It has been the author's experience that many high-achieving boys in junior high school write a garland, slightly backhand script like the one shown in Figure 179. Many add flourishes such as circled i-dots, usually

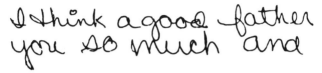

Fig. 179

associated with girls. The writing in total is less free and easy than that of the less inhibited youngsters.

The father's absence from home, his frequent abdication of authority to the mother, his failure to relate adequately to his son, all have contributed to the decline of masculinity in the traditional sense. Long hair, uni-sex, homosexuality, drug-taking, all are calling attention to the growing ranks of alienated and rejected young.

On the positive side: in our modern technology, aggressive "masculine" traits may be more dangerous than useful. The need to dominate, and to acquire at all costs, are not necessarily advantageous to society in the long run. More "feminine" traits such as nurturing, sympathy and cooperation may be required to maintain an equable social order. A new balance between the sexes may prove advantageous to the entire world.

According to some psychoanalysts, the balance of male-female envy appears to be shifting. Freud theorized that women envied the male penis. Today, women are less envious of men and men, perhaps, more envious of women. Maybe it was not the penis, per se, but the dominant and independent male social role that Freud's Victorian Age female envied. At any rate, when we see changes in the roles of the sexes, we see changes in total attitude within the self-image.

What is ahead? We can be sure there will be further change. We can be reasonably certain that a society which will be in the best interests of both male and female, and the children produced, will call for cooperation. Building a sound future demands initiative, self-discipline, and mutual respect. Will these factors be evident in future school-model handwriting forms? Only time will tell. Whatever the changes may be, the expressive movement of the script will reflect the self-image and social environment of each writer, no matter what his age.

Wide possibilities exist for the use of handwriting analysis. But before such possibilities can be fully utilized, professional graphology must filter through the atmosphere of entertainment or cultism which too often surrounds primary efforts in understanding the self-image. Just as they are more widely used abroad, graphological techniques may serve as counseling aids through which clinical judgment may be reached or further valid testing be devised. Graphology may serve to bridge a communication gap in counseling.

There is "more than the message" in the "crystallized gesture" of handwriting. And the "more" suggests that the uniqueness, beauty and integrity of the person are his, and the world's, most valuable possessions.

PART IV

CHANGING THE
SELF-IMAGE

Chapter 1

YOUR SELF-IMAGE AND GRAPHOTHERAPY

It has been the basic premise of this book that the way you write your personal pronoun *I* reflects your self-image, the manner in which you consciously and unconsciously view yourself. We have seen that as a person changes his view of himself in response to internal or external circumstances, his personal pronoun also changes in subtle ways discernible to an experienced graphologist. Such a change in the written pp*I* in response to a deepened and enlarged view of herself is most dramatically shown in the case of Bette Mae, described in chapter 3, part III. As Bette Mae was confronted with hitherto unexplored parts of herself after the unexpected death of her husband, the character of her pp*I* gradually changed from a moderate, conventional pp*I* into an angular, printed pp*I*, reflecting her growing independence and creatively expanded self-image.

If a person's personal pronoun *I* can change in response to modifications of his self-image, it seems plausible to assume that a person's self-image may be

253

changed in response to modifications of his written, personal pronoun *I*. This assumption actually constitutes the basic impetus of *grapho*therapy, a therapeutic system that seeks to improve an individual's personality by inducing a set of changes in his handwriting.

Like the study of psychology in general, graphotherapy has a short history. The treatment of personality through consciously made changes in writing was first suggested by European psychologists. The term "graphotherapy" came into being around 1930 in the Paris Academy of Medicine through Dr. Edgar Berillon, psychologist and authority at the time on mental diseases. His treatment technique rested upon his belief that the conduit established between the cortex of the brain and the hand via the nervous system is a two-way process. According to Dr. Berillon, imprinting qualities between graphological gestures and the brain are reversible. He termed his treatment "psychotherapie graphique" meaning that treatment (therapy) combines both mental (psychic) and physical (graphic) processes.

This system was tested clinically at the Sorbonne in Paris between 1929 and 1931 by Dr. Pierre Janet and Professor Charlest Henry. The late French graphologist, Paule de Sainte Columbe, was the consulting graphologist at the time. Experiments appeared to confirm that the system of graphotherapy could give impressive results. In 1948 Dr. Pierre Menard, a former student of Dr. Janet, published a notable book on the subject of graphotherapeutics. Although Paule de Sainte Columbe had an active group in California prior to his death, graphotherapy has received scant attention in America.

The practice of graphotherapy includes a plan of systematically modifying handwriting according to instructions applied by a competent graphotherapist. Graphotherapy undertakes to *retrain* specific writing gestures which offer the potential to strengthen specific habits of thought. This principle has much in common with learning theory: only consistent practice develops proficiency. Ultimately the gestures' "meanings" are unconsciously assimilated, so that responses are made more or less automatically. In graphotherapy, the goal theoretically is achieved when the desired change in the handwriting has become internalized and "normal" for the writer. A superficial copying of structural form alone cannot change negative thinking regarding the self; underlying elements of *rhythm, size, slant, pressure* and other factors must be incorporated consciously in the writing in appropriate sequence. It must be done under adequate supervision which takes into account the capacities of the client.

Common examples of the practice of graphotherapy involve the repetition of graphic symbols such as the *garland, arcade, angle* and *thread.* Characteristic associations accompanying such specific graphic patterns have been tested at various times with respect to the emotions engendered by writing them as well as by observing them.[1]

1. In his article "Sentic Cycles—the Seven Passions at Your Finger-tips" (*Psychology Today,* May, 1972), Manfred Clyne writes: "We may consider that there is a common brain program for specific

Another method in graphotherapy is to have the counselee copy inspirational sentences, accompanied also by the altering of specific letters within words. To the author's knowledge, specific use of the personal pronoun *I* as a focus of graphic effort has not ordinarily been practiced. It would appear that the personal pronoun accompanied by one or two words is adequate for experimental purposes.

In the graphotherapeutic process, the *I* symbol would initially be only "drawn." After practice, spontaneous writing develops and the desirable factors are incorporated within the self. The self-esteem and awareness of the counselee are usually increased, especially if appropriate counseling accompanies the practice. In such a never-ending cycle of stimulus-response, change appears inevitable within the continuum of physical imprinting.

It must be emphasized that a sudden change in the form of the *I* usually is not desirable. The individuality of the writer must be respected, and only after a series of graduated exercises is the writer ordinarily ready and

---

emotions that determines the *character* of [a] movement and its precise time course, regardless of the particular body movement that expresses it. . . ." Experiments suggest that there is a specific dynamic form of action underlying the expression of such emotion, and that the dynamic character of this action form is probably universal, unlearned and genetically programmed. Anger, grief, hate, love, joy, sexual desire and reverence all produced distinct muscle movements. According to Mr. Clyne's article, this spectrum of emotions is precisely programmed by the brain. The programming is different for different emotions. Such discoveries appear to provide an empirical framework for the principles of graphotherapy discussed in this and the following chapter.

capable of assuming behavioral changes. Gradual modification of the ego symbol is best accompanied by alterations of other letters, also, as recommended by a qualified graphologist who is trained in counseling and educationally qualified to work with others in the field of psychology.

Chapter 2

CASE HISTORIES IN CHANGING THE SELF-IMAGE

The following case histories in changing the self-image are all drawn from the author's experience with graphotherapy. The specific personal goals were different in each case, but in general each counselee expressed the desire to increase his sense of worth along with the ability to relate more meaningfully and successfully with others.

Counseling procedures adhered primarily to Adlerian principles of mutual exploration of the family constellation, early recollections, mistaken and self-defeating apperceptions, and a definitive description of the counselee's life style. Procedures also involved each counselee's initially writing a number of sentences which included personal pronouns. All met privately with the therapist-counselor for brief weekly sessions consisting of exercises and evaluation of progress. All exercises involved the daily use of carbon paper copies for estimates of writing pressure.

While each case assignment was different at different

times, the same principle of morning and evening practice sessions applied to all. After initial evaluation and checking of each assignment weekly or twice-weekly, the therapist suggested specific changes in various elements of the written *I* and accompanying words. The counselees' feelings while doing treatment exercises were discussed with the therapist. All counselees described similar changes of attitude while making certain strokes; for example, *garland* emphasis elicited feelings of relaxation, while definite *angles* produced a feeling of control. Consistency and concentration, particularly with respect to maintenance of pressure, proved difficult in the beginning. Spontaneity and balanced rhythm, however, increased with practice.

Each writer was requested to repeat his daily exercises for a certain number of pages, checking for correct carbon pressure after each page. Assignments generally took no more than twenty minutes two times a day. Six elements were emphasized: pressure, size, slant, pattern (including scope, angularity, elaboration and zonal emphasis), rhythm and word relationships. Materials used were an 8-by-11 inch lined writing tablet, carbon paper, and cartridge or ballpoint pen.

The possibility of traumatic effect during the graphotherapeutic process may be illustrated by an unusual incident during the course of the program. At an early point in her therapy, one counselee decided to hurry along her progress by altering her personal pronoun in a drastic manner without first discussing it with the therapist. The form of her new *I* was different from the form of her usual

I. Coincidentally or not, the results were disquieting. In her own words:

> When I woke up that morning I was suddenly conscious that there was someone—an actual form, a "thing," standing right beside me. It was dressed in a garment I could actually see. . . . I could not see the figure's face. . . . This had never happened to me before. I determined to proceed as normally as possible throughout the day. As the day went along, the figure was somehow with me all the time. I was not really afraid. . . . I sensed that it was guiding me, in a way. . . ."

Counseling naturally proceeded along lines appropriate to this particular instance. The situation was resolved. It must be emphatically stated again, however, that graphotherapy must only be attempted by persons trained in procedures which are not detrimental to the welfare of their clients.

The following case histories are brief reports of happenings in the author's experience with graphotherapy and/or counseling. They are not to be construed as rules of procedure but as mere guidelines in the general graphotherapeutic process.

Case Histories

Ms. A is a middle-aged grade-school teacher with an advanced degree. She is right-handed. Her therapy included daily writing exercises plus twice-weekly counseling sessions involving exploration of family constellation, early recollections and a description of her life style.[1]

Ms. A, a friendly, intelligent and disciplined woman, entered graphotherapy and counseling in order to increase her communication skills. Although she has been able to share many of her problems with priests and others within her religious order, repeated frustrations involving administration and dealing with progressively unruly classes during the past two years has caused her great concern. Her expressed goal at the beginning of therapy was to reveal her feelings without hurting others or feeling guilty.

Fig. 180

The carefully spaced, conforming garland aspects of Ms. A's writing, shown in Figure 180, reveals a persistent individual with a need for order—a person who is discriminating and enjoys handling detail. Her organizational ability reinforces a methodical approach to problem-solving. The writing exhibits a strong need to please others and appreciation of spiritual and ethical values. However, a conforming viewpoint allows little scope for originality and there appears to be a general lack of enthusiasm.

1. Only a few of the many writing samples from the writing exercises are shown in the following pages.

Diagnosis of the ppI:

Pressure: *Displaced.*
Size: *Large.*
Slant: *Vertical, counter-dominant to text.*
Pattern: *Pictorial, arcade, elaborated.*
Zonal Emphasis: *Middle and lower.*
Rhythm: *Sporadic.*

At first glance, Ms. A's copybook pp*I* appears to add little to the analysis. Nevertheless, the emotional content found within this conventionally formed ego symbol reveals a number of unresolved inner conflicts. The immediate key factor is the displacement of writing pressure, indicating a depletion of vitality and an imbalance of inner control—a fighting within the self. In several instances, when the *I* pressure appeared normal, as in Figure 181, a closer scrutiny of carbon copies revealed the true displacement—a light downstroke and a heavy upstroke.

I'm not sure

Fig. 181

It must be recalled that repression in handwriting is represented graphically by a chronic muscular tension and imbalance which cuts off the natural rhythmic order and disturbs the dynamics of contraction and release. Such physical contradictions cannot be integrated psychologically any more than contradictory ideas can be harmoniously and actively resolved. This reversal of pressure takes its toll in a chronic strain which most likely will express itself in anger. Such a counter-impulse within the written ego symbol offers the clue that Ms. A carries a heavy load of unresolved stress. A dichotomy of pressure often implies suppression of feelings, causing tension over unconscious elements which the individual cannot identify. The occasional appearance of a pointed and/or looped male image within her ego symbol is another key factor suggesting Ms. A's hidden tension. Such strokes suggest possible disappointment, anger or concern regarding a male authority figure.

On the basis of the diagnosis of Ms. A's written ego symbol, it was the therapist's goal to have her enlarge and emphasize her self-awareness, to increase her enthusiasm, to encourage her decision-making and to decrease her need to control others. In this way, a lessening of anger and inner rebellion could result.

Beneath the conventional surface of her pp*I* lay the writer's use of social distance to avoid feelings of humiliation, and a notion that overt rebellion would be futile. Further questioning revealed one possible origin of early conflict concerning the written *I*– she recalled that while learning to write, the penmanship teacher corrected her for forming the capital *I* backwards. Thereafter, she wrote the letter properly, but displacement of pressure could be interpreted as representing a sense of lost autonomy, plus covert rebellion.

Family constellation: Ms. A was the youngest of three

little girls when her mother died. She developed an increasingly deep impression of loss over this event. Her father remarried and some years later several other children were born. Both parents were strict, demanding and hard-working. There was little real intimacy within the group as a whole. Growing up, Ms. A saw her worth primarily as the family baby-sitter, with few outside opportunities for friends. Her relationship with her father was distant. As time went on, Ms. A achieved far less than her scholastic abilities would indicate. During counseling, Ms. A wrote:

> I have never before brought to the surface, or at least have never verbalized, my feelings that my father was disappointed in my lack of success in music, in the business world, in social circles and in my perception of his needs when he was ill. I have never realized that in infancy and early childhood I was, in a way, abandoned by him, as he was preoccupied with sorrow and struggle in his very effort to provide a home for himself and for us. . . . This reinforced self-pity in me.

Ms. A also expressed the awareness that she had been jealous of her father's seemingly great self-confidence and assurance, as well as angry with his insensitivity to her feelings of inadequacy.

The ideas which evolved for Ms. A during graphotherapy included the following:

- Failure as a pattern is not inevitable and not necessarily the best frame of reference for me. It has been a pattern in my life.
- For much of my life, I have seen imperfection as a source of rejection and have kept trying to be perfect and hide my imperfections rather than face them.
- Guilt feelings are a warning. I must bring them to the surface as soon as I become aware of them. I must find the cause and accept the cure.

Mistaken and self-defeating apperceptions from the past which were dominating much of Ms. A's thinking included viewing life as sad. She had a need to control others, juxtaposed with a need to please and to conform without openly expressing her feelings. She said, "The worst thing is to be misunderstood."

At the end of graphotherapy and counseling regarding her life style, Ms. A expressed the following insights:

I feel a new depth of freedom from fears. Our discussions have confirmed my conclusion that my frequent outbursts of anger, which have been my most regular and troublesome failing in the past year, were indications of a deep-seated rebellion of long standing.

The considerable assets of Ms. A include the courage to face change, integrity of purpose, a developing sense of humor and emerging enthusiasm for what life holds for her. Recognizing that she has real ability in organizing materials and projects may help her future career in Special Education.

Graphological Treatment Program:

Pressure: *Reduce carbon imprint from four to two carbons; eliminate displaced pressure.*
Size: *Become aware of relative height of letters.*
Slant: *Emphasize consistent rightward movement in harmony with text.*
Pattern: *Moderate elaboration and zonal emphasis.*
Rhythm: *Practice contraction-release.*
Word relationship: *Narrow the personal pronoun's distance from text.*

Progressive writing samples:

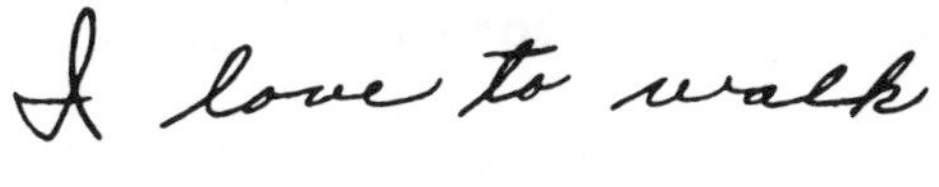

Fig. 182

Althought writing pressure looks normal, scrutiny of the carbon copy reveals displacement in the upstroke of the *I*.

Fig. 183

Getting in touch with her feelings involved the use of

angles. Lessening of writing pressure may produce feelings of anxiety or loss of control which is counteracted by such angular strokes.

I am I am I am

Fig. 184

Garlands and closer contact with the text improved fluidity of writing. Eliminating the extra loop in the *I* simplified the pattern.

I am I am I am

Fig. 185

Correcting displaced pressure demanded utmost concentration and resulted in uneven tremor.

I am total I

Fig. 186

A feeling of release is emphasized through horizontal expansion.

I and I and I

Fig. 187

Angles and retraced d-stems helped control. Even slant emphasized inner rhythm.

until I was sure

Fig. 188

Increased positive writing elements.

Female College Student

Ms. B is a 22-year-old graduate student. She is right-handed. No counseling was given in connection with her program of graphotherapy.

something I think

Fig. 189

Ms. B's careful, deliberate writing, shown in Figure 189, echoes much of the discriminating self-image revealed by her personal pronoun. Although the writer is highly emotional, she values and exhibits personal control, dignity and self-discipline. Refinement and suppression of inappropriate behavior are in keeping with her conscientious attention to detail and practical common sense. Socially adept, but inwardly shy, she wants to be needed, has a strong nesting instinct and finds pleasure in the role as homemaker. Material niceties appeal to her and she appreciates design, form and color.

Diagnosis of the ppI:

Pressure: *Light.*
Size: *Small to moderate.*

Slant: *Rightward.*
Pattern: *Pictorial with angle.*
Rhythm: *Slow.*
Word Relationship: *Crowded.*

Ms. B's pp*I* offers further insight into her interest and talent in the female role of homemaker. The straightened upward stroke and top angle of her unusually shaped ego symbol suggest sensitivity to criticism and domination by female authority figures. She has a strong need for independence and for establishing her own way of doing things. The loop within the male figure hints at her vulnerability to disappointments, her sensitivity to playing second fiddle, and her feelings that at times she compares unfavorably with others.

Ms. B's goals were to be less controlling of others, less competitive, and less in need always of being in the right. She also expressed a desire to be more accepting of both herself and others. Further needs suggested by her written ego symbol called for increased flexibility and spontaneous expression, as well as a more objective view of the male and female roles.

Graphological treatment program:

Pressure: *Increase.*
Size: *Increase.*
Slant: *Maintain.*
Pattern: *Moderate the form, with alternatives to arcades and angles.*

Rhythm: *Increase with speed.*
Word Relationship: *Enlarge distance between* I *and text.*

Progressive writing samples:

Fig. 190

Conscious effort made to press paper harder to triple carbon number. Change of arcade to garland strokes.

Fig. 191

Counselee asked to experiment with different *I*, increasing and straightening male symbol to the right and eliminating loop.

Fig. 192

Final simplification of the *I*, with more space between words.

Male College Student

Mr. C is a 22-year-old college student. He is right-handed. No counseling was given in connection with his therapeutic exercises.

I feel happiest

Fig. 193

Mr. C's writing, shown in Figure 193, suggests refined tastes, literary interests, capacity for observation and psychological insight. Fluency of verbal expression is superior, and the writer possesses an abundance of charm and openness to new experiences. He has a noticeable appreciation of color, texture, design and art forms. His good physical coordination is emphasized by the swing of his writing.

*Diagnosis of the pp*I*:*

Pressure: *Light, with horizontal displacement.*
Size: *Small.*
Slant: *Reclined.*
Pattern: *Pictorial.*
Rhythm: *Uneven release.*
Word Relationship: *Wide separation from text.*

In spite of the general appearance of fluidity, a hesitancy to move ahead is revealed by the reclined, rocking-horse pp*I*. Mr. C's self-image appears hindered to some degree by his deep feelings of vulnerability and his high priority on comfort which necessitates avoidance of undue stress. The price paid for such hesitation to move forward is an increasing sense of unproductiveness, a fact suggested by the writer's displacement of pressure. The lack of a well defined male image within his written ego symbol also suggests emotional separation and alienation from the father image.

The stated goal of Mr. C was to avoid the "yes—but" rationalizing approach. Restlessness, his need for expanding goals, and dependence upon winning recognition from others are at odds with his inclination toward passivity. Further therapeutic goals therefore included increased decisiveness and sense of control, heightened awareness of his unconscious, representational behavior and accentuation of a positive male image.

Graphological treatment program:

Pressure: *Increase.*
Size: *Enlarge.*
Slant: *Pull to vertical.*
Pattern: *Increase angular movements.*
Rhythm: *Improve through contraction-release emphasis.*
Word Relationship: *Narrow distance from I to text.*

Progressive writing samples:

I am I am
I am I am

Fig. 194

Increasing pressure from one carbon to four,
accenting an easy rhythm.

I am
I am

Fig. 195

Move the *I* closer to accompanying word; accent
garland final.

I am attracted

Fig. 196

Increase height of *I*; lengthen and strengthen both cursive and printed male symbols; retracing of t- and d-stems.

I wanted

Fig. 197

Vertical emphasis with angular strokes.

Fig. 198

Personal pronoun *I* now sits squarely on the base of the writing line, although pressure displacement still needs correction.

Female High School Teacher

Ms. D is a 44-year-old high school teacher and doctoral candidate. She is right-handed. Her therapy consisted of twice-daily writing exercise plus twice-a-week counseling session.

The expressed goal of this attractive counselee was to "get off dead center," since she was finding it difficult to proceed with her studies and complete her doctoral thesis.

Fig. 199

Ms. D's refined handwriting of high-form level, shown in Figure 199, indicates a sensitive and highly charged emotional nature which requires much expenditure of nervous energy for endurance. There are indications of deeply felt spiritual yearnings, a need to accomplish and to be intellectually engaged. Acute sensitivity to her physical environment, and awareness of music, form and color heighten her vulnerability to swings of mood. Fastidiousness, determination and a need to win, all point to the writer's exclusion of inner feelings in favor of goal-directedness. Accompanying this is a tendency to have too many irons in the fire at the same time and to procrastinate. There is some need to defy, and, although she is capable of great charm and humor, she is highly critical of both herself and others.

Diagnosis of the ppI:

Pressure: *Heavy.*
Size: *Tall, narrow.*
Slant: *Rightward.*
Pattern: *Linear.*
Rhythm: *Sweeping but erratic.*
Word Relationship: *Distant.*

Ms. D's narrow ego symbol indicates a certain inflexibility and guardedness, representative of a very private person. Covering strokes suggests a denial of feelings as well as shutting out of psychic awareness. The angular appearance of her personal pronoun *I* is significant of the writer's pervasive need to orient herself according to certain rigid value judgments. This, it may be surmised, would cause her to proceed on private assumptions not necessarily shared by others. A feeling of alienation from others is indicated, with ambivalent feelings concerning those in authority. She has superior standards and a need in some degree to separate herself from deep emotional ties with others. A key factor in Ms. D's written *I* is the angled "swords' point" at which the male and female symbols meet. This suggests the writer has been exposed to rigid, perhaps constricted and contrary viewpoints regarding the male and female roles. It may be surmised that opposing viewpoints in this regard as well as parental conflicts would have concerned the writer. A sense of competition with male authority figures may be expected to ensue from such experiences.

Further treatment goals for Ms. D included heightened awareness of her unconscious symbolic behavior which represent and express her conflicting ideas about male and female roles; developing and expressing congruence between her inner and outward self; recognizing the presence of unexamined hostility, and lessening the need to over-burden herself.

Family constellation: Ms. D is a squeezed middle child in a family of four; she and her closest sister were only a year apart in age, in between an older brother and a favored younger sister. There was considerable friction between the parents, both of whom were professionally educated, strong-minded and competitive. The children were generally allied against the father in the family power struggle. Ms. D inwardly felt that she could never win in competition with her brother for the affection of her mother. Her father, ostensibly the head of the family, was out of touch with his children. Open expression of sadness, sexuality and female strength were generally kept at a minimum or unadmitted in the family circle.

In evaluating Ms. D's early recollections, a number of self-defeating concepts appeared. These included the assumption that others were better recognized unless she could prove herself; life was competitive; boys (men) were distant, not to be counted on and appreciated more than girls; feelings were to be ignored; she was more an observer than a participant. Among Ms. D's considerable assets were her desire for honesty, her kindness, initiative, capacity for hard work, and intellectual curiosity.

Ms. D's final goals, formulated during the course of therapy, included the following:

> . . . to strengthen the ability to direct myself, finishing projects, integrating my powers; to let other people live and not try to boss them, to strengthen my ability to listen to words, nuances, situations; to be more sensitive to other people's feelings.

At the end of counseling, Ms. D wrote down the following list of specific problems which had seen improvement since she began graphotherapy:

- I have more order in my relationship with a particular man. . . .
- I have made more progress in finishing things.
- I can cope better with my university project.
- I handle guilt feelings better—another big thing. I

feel more able to make decisions.

- I am more conscious of being on time. I get more library books back when they are due. My work is becoming more orderly.
- I can see some way that I could improve my relationship with Mother.
- I can at times ride my bike with one hand. This may not be important, but I like to see my coordination improving.
- I think my emotional "shock absorbers" are improving. I recover earlier from personal disappointments then I would have done two months ago. I am not conscious of any rankling bitterness, but on the contrary, feel I have learned from my past disappointments.

Graphological treatment program:

Pressure: *Reduce.*
Size: *Enlarge appropriate to surrounding words.*
Slant: *Minimize rightward trend.*
Pattern: *Lessen angularity, eliminate elaboration, minimize lower zone placement.*
Rhythm: *Practice contraction-release.*
Word Relationship: *Narrow distance between I and text.*

Progressive writing samples:

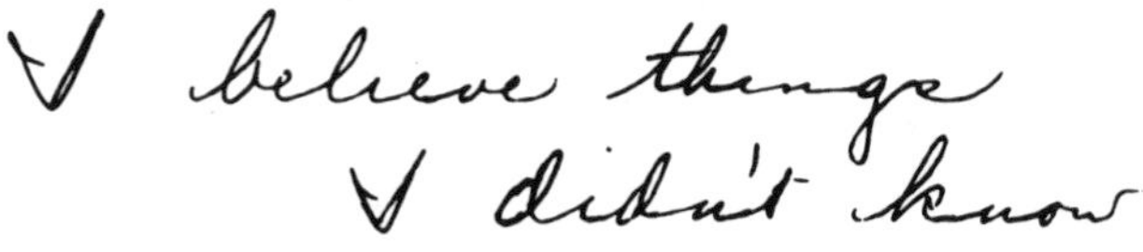

I believe things
I didn't know

Fig. 200

Carbon imprint reduced from five to two carbon copies. Writing tension lessened as pressure is lessened.

I am I am I

Fig. 201

Garland strokes emphasized in adjacent word.

I told I told I told

Fig. 202

Focus on placing *I* squarely on baseline helps; female symbol enlarged; t-stem retraced for control.

I wanted I wanted

Fig. 203

Difficulty with displacement of pressure evident.

I wanted   I wanted

Fig. 204

Increasing male symbol while retaining correct pressure is difficult.

Fig. 205

Practice in scope and rhythm control.

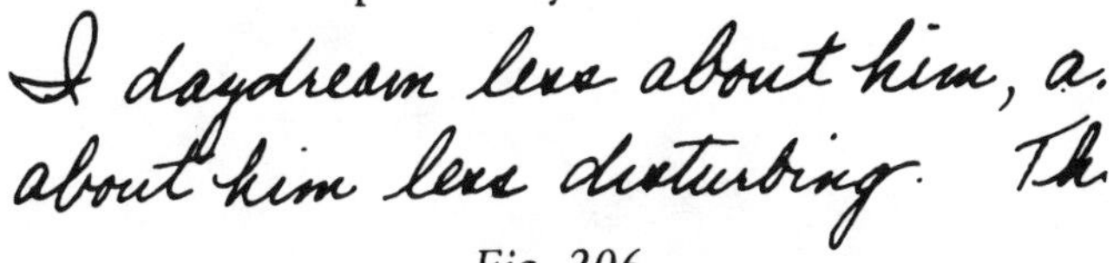

I daydream less about him, a.
about him less disturbing. Th.

Fig. 206

Word relationship improved; zonal emphasis is corrected.

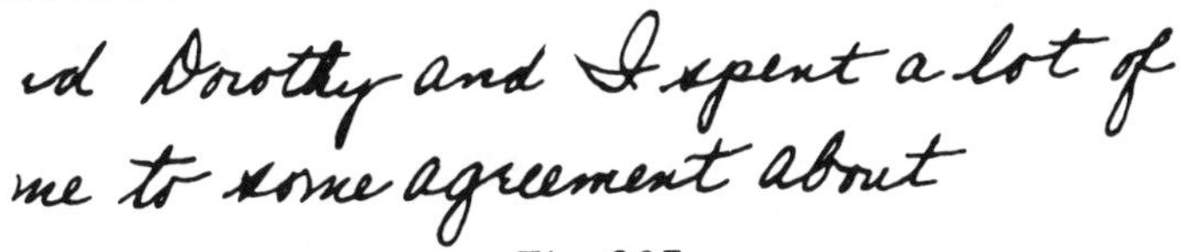

d Dorothy and I spent a lot of
me to some agreement about

Fig. 207

Note balanced size of *I* with other letters; rhythm, slant, pattern, word relationship and pressure improved.

Chapter 3

Symbolism and the Why of the I

In this final chapter, let us recapitulate the essence of the relationship of handwriting to man. The act of writing is a distinctively human activity. Not only is it distinctively human, it is also specifically unique to each individual. Its individuality is often recognized even by the most casual observer. It is affected by and reflects to some degree—although yet unmeasured and barely known—the physical condition of the writer. In short, handwriting is an element of the indivisible whole that makes up a person; it is another ingredient in the dynamic unity which is part and parcel of each one of us. It is a mirror that speaks even from a distance of the submerged inner self.

The question most often asked of a graphologist is "How scientific is it?" Before addressing ourselves to this question, however, we must first ask another question. Can the term "science" be properly applied to the investigations of social psychology, perception, creativity, learning, aesthetics or other phenomena relevant to what are essentially

283

human activities? Is there actually a discipline in which such an activity as handwriting can be placed and measured? What has been termed the idolatry of science in our age has come up with surprisingly little firm evidence concerning psychology as a whole after more than a century of effort. Certainly at the present time there is vast disagreement, some minor, some profoundly divergent, among professionals concerned with human behavior. It is questionable if graphology can be or should be placed in the position of any but an empirical study. Consensual validation may prove to be the most meaningful. Such common agreement accords with common sense. Nevertheless, scientific methods of investigation must be pursued if graphology is to be accepted in academia.

Long ago handwriting was considered to be divinely inspired. As a communication device it was kept firmly in the hands of priests, who recognized its value in maintaining power for the privileged few. At one time it was a criminal act to teach slaves to read and write in this country. The power of the written word is well known, and power has accrued to those able to utilize it. Perhaps it is not surprising that the very act of writing was sacrosanct. Some glimmer of its magnitude still lingers in the cuneiform or picture writing from ages past. The symbolic meaning of form and space passes from generation to generation, and is continually expressed not only in the art but in the writing forms of each generation.

The study of graphology and the expressive gestures of handwriting offer promises of new insights into the vast territory between the physiological and the psychological.

The study of handwriting analysis is concerned with symbolic communication. It is accepted graphologically that various aspects of handwriting bear relationship to male and female orientation. Symbolically, the left side of the paper environment relates to the past, or mother. The right side relates to the future, or father. Traces of parental and other male-female influences have been established through such graphic factors as directional pressure, form level, left/right trendings, extreme circularity or angularity, slant, incomplete or unusually formed or placed letters, margins, and types of connection. The question of *why* there are male and female influences within the personal pronoun *I* and *why* the female symbol appears first in the copybook stroke involve concepts of such space and form orientation as well as the writer's concepts of self and sexual identity.

Personal symbolism is created when imagination is integrated through experiences involving ourself and others. Layers of meaning exist in given forms which appear visible to individuals who are able through previous experiences and background encounters to assimilate and recognize them. Such meanings are relevant to the fact that the shape of the pp*I* will often change as the self-image changes.

Hand motions have translated common symbols from time immemorial, from the cortex, to cave walls, stone, bark, cloth and paper. It is our nature to communicate through hand or body motion as well as language. Body language is recognized and transmitted, for example, in art—specifically in the Orient by calligraphy students who are instructed to "think" the emotion or quality they wish to portray and project upon paper. Transference of mental and emotional energy integrates muscularly into particular expressive movements whereby the flight of the hawk, the fury of the lion and other dynamic concepts are caught by the artist who projects these tensions visually. Miniscule shadings within each stroke bear significant meaning for both artist and viewer.

Symbolic graphic patterns develop somewhere within the unconscious mind. Even viewing individual patterns we find many times a universal, underlying consistency of emotional response which has not been specifically "taught" but has common dimensions intuitively recognized. For example, in past and present societies it appears that circle shapes embrace the concept of the "all." The cross mandala signifies unity throughout the world. The figure eight, horizontally placed, appears as an "infinity" symbol in many diverse cultures. It is common among children of all known cultures to begin drawing attempts with roughly sketched circles representing the totality of a being, whether animal or human. These circles later acquire, in a progressive manner, stick arms and legs, "active" straight lines.

The two concepts of circle and straight, soft and hard, are fundamental to the forming of the personal pronoun which represents the self. The self which knows experience is defined psychologically as possessing both male and female attributes. The American written symbol expresses both the circular motion and straight lines in copybook form as a general rule. Graphic strokes blend with art forms in male-female symbolism; curved lines represent a "soft" intent, and tension and activity are commonly associated with straight or angled motion. Anthropogists and artists are familiar with totem figures representing the female which possess significantly exaggerated round breasts and belly. In expressing the "all" it is not unlikely that in some mysterious way, children delve backward into earliest tribal memories, the collective unconscious and the anima-animus espoused by Carl Jung.

Just as the formation of personality proceeds in progressive stages which may or may not become impeded, the logic of handwriting analysis suggests that disruption of form is particularly significant and related to such influences.

Dual action exists in the broadest sense as we write our self-image. The written ego symbol expresses the principle that we are continuously relating to others unconsciously even when most intimately committed to the self. Just as the private self-concept reflects an individual's previous experience and capacities, common logic suggests that the expressive movements of writing reflect something of the background incorporating the most intimate experiences of beginning life—the family unit.

There are three main factors influencing the hypothesis that male and female symbols exist within the *I* in the particular order established. The first factor is that the mother-child relationship is the initial and primary influence ordinarily met by the emerging conscious self. The second factor relates to the combination of "soft" and "hard" strokes found in the written *I*. The third factor is the recognition by graphologists that male and female influences are found in other graphic strokes and their placement on the writing background.

Physically and psychologically the infant first experiences the mother, bonded within the circle of breast and arm just as within the rounded womb and belly. Even biology adds its own weight to the primary quality of the female relationship, for we find that the ovum within the mother, the egg which receives the sperm of the male, contains an X chromosome. It is female in essence, for it is the male chromosome carried by an individual sperm which gives an embryo its male sex when egg and sperm unite. Unless the sperm contains a Y chromosome, the infant conceived will be born female.

Philosophic consideration suggests there is a universal logic to human behavior and graphic association. According to anthropolists James Frazer and Margaret Mead, coitus was not associated with childbirth in the earliest stages of humankind's development. Human fecundity was not understood. Because only women gave birth, producing after their own kind, the female appeared to be revered as givers-of-life. The males' part was unknown. Joseph Campbell, in *The Masks of God: Primitive Mythology*, writes:

> "There can be no doubt that in the very earliest ages of human history the magical force and wonder of the female was no less a marvel than the universe itself, and this gave to women a prodigious power . . . It is, in fact, most remarkable how many primitive hunting races have the legend of a still more primitive

age than their own, in which the women were the sole possessors of the magical art." **p. 315**

In Mesopotamia the Goddess Ninlil was revered for having provided the understanding of planting and harvesting. In prehistory as well as in early historic times, religions existed in which people revered their supreme creator as female.

Mythologies regarding "The Great Mother" are found around the world. The Divine Ancestress has been worshipped from the beginnings of the Neolithic periods of 7,000 B.C. until the closing of the last Goddess temple around A.D. 500. Some authorities extend goddess worship as far back as the Upper Paleolithic age of around 25,000 B.C. Concepts of a female deity as Wise Creatures of the Universe and civilization run throughout diverse cultures in spite of more recent patriarchal images. The mother figure and its power and influence cannot really be discounted in the part it plays in human personality development.

In India the Goddess Sarasvati was honored as the inventor of the original alphabet. It was the Goddess Nidaba in Sumer who was esteemed as the inventor of the clay tablets and the art of writing. In Celtic Ireland, named for the Goddess Eire, the Goddess Brigit was honored as patron deity of language.

While the eternal mother is found throughout ancient cultures in the role of prophetess and conciliator, the eternal father encompasses the ideas of action and power within the every-day world. We associate the masculine concept with a figure striving to extend his realm in a dynamic manner, just as we generally and traditionally find associations with the female quality in areas of spirituality and the supernatural.

It is still culturally accepted in most countries that the passivity of the feminine is complemented and supported by the activity of the male figure. From primordial times it appears that motherhood implies accepting, sheltering and nurturing aspects of life and fatherhood implies supplying and defending. Role models exist which are felt by children throughout the world which emphasize such qualities.

Role models which are so dominant in so much of the world definitely affect what it means to be male or female in society, even when roles are changing. The self-image which springs from such early beginnings, which may include the collective unconscious, is based in some part upon the male and female role-model concept. Biology, history and psychological considerations merge in the study of the ego symbol.

It is generally accepted by psychologists that children of both sexes ideally tend to regard the father as a model of courage and strength which they need for full development of such qualities in themselves. Besides being a vital factor in personality development for both boys and girls, the father figure also provides the child with a sense of the importance of the every-day world beyond the limits of the home. Such terminology as "fatherland" implies a certain measure of strength and emotional stamina necessary to maintain a specific identity. In similar fashion, connotations of drive and energy are implied within the masculine ideal.

Psychologically, after the primary relationship with

the mother, the relationship with the father, the family system itself, and the larger world begin. The child begins to establish his or her identity.

A healthy social identity appears to be significantly related to a healthy connection with the father. Social elements are to be found within the middle zone of handwriting; for example, social feelings of "isolation" are believed to be particularly related to split letters, wide distances between words, and to letters which should touch the baseline but do not. The father symbol is likewise within the middle zone of the pp*I*.

Angular connections suggest that the writer experienced repression from a dominant father figure, according to some graphologists. Garland connections are considered to be more feminine and emphasize the relationship to the mother. Excessive circularity has been equated with unfulfilled oral needs or a basic disappointment concerning the amount of love received from the mother or surrogate. All of the above factors correlated symbolically with the structure of the *I* and support the hypothesis concerning male/female influences within the *I*. Such elements found within the handwriting text will generally be found within the written personal pronoun.

The *I* pinpoints the general handwriting qualities which can be quickly noted and considered by analyst and client together, especially where counseling is indicated. The question is not whether the ego symbol is "primary" or "secondary" but to what use it can be put in the service of graphology. The written pp*I*, differentiated from the capital *I*, leads us quickly to the root of personality. It may complement, supplement, or perhaps offer a counter-dominant which bears investigation and points the way to a deep-seated conflict within the individual. The pp*I* is a springboard to understanding, offering clues from the past to present-day relationships.

The six elements which modify all handwriting—height, length, slant, pressure, scope, angularity and elaboration—are significantly condensed within the pp*I*. The ego symbol also becomes a metaphor of graphic male and female qualities which suggest receptivity and aggression. Certain strokes seem to have the capacity to be representative of both empathy and projection. Both hard and soft strokes would theoretically exist in American copybook models since both qualities optimally appear in an egalitarian society.

In this regard, the structure of the *I* is significant: the high arched dome of the female symbol lies rooted in the instinctual and physical area of lower zone. The graphic loop moves through the middle zone area of daily affairs, practical events and social concerns into the upper areas of ethical and spiritual concerns. The male image is represented by a curve from right to left, then straight thrust stroke which initially moves from the left (female area). In this context it may be said to be relating to the past and to early maternal influences which are necessarily relevant to sexual encounter.

The *soft* line of the male symbol changes into the *hard* stroke as its motion changes to the right area traditionally associated with the future and with the male. Palmer and Zaner-Blozer copybook forms at this point junction with the female image. In the interaction, a tri-angular or wedge-shaped area of integration is formed. The male stroke then continues, after penetrating the area of integration, and moves rightward toward the area of the future within the paper environment. Interestingly, *cunei-form* writing is the wedge-shaped writing used by ancient Assyrians, Babylonians and Persians. The word "cuneiform" stems originally from early Assyrian words referring specifically to the female.

To summarize: First, we have the starting point of the copybook capital *I* slightly below the baseline of every-day experience, a possible metaphor of the self beginning below the conscious level of physical being. Second, still in terms of metaphor, the protective female (mother) loop takes the infant upward through the daily routine (middle zone) into the spiritual-ethical concern area (upper zone). Concepts of virtue, holiness and purity have traditionally been associated with the best of mothering and motherhood. The curving motion at the apex suggests qualities of flex-ibility and yielding which are culturally accepted aspects of feminine behavior. We find the total picture of the ego symbol *I* includes a balanced starting point, then a retro-spective attitude reaching backward and upwards for past influences, and finally a forward motion to the right which includes room for growth and future expansion and effort toward others.

It is not the intent of the writer to suggest that one factor is the more important. We must also emphasize that an *I* by itself may contain poitive and/or negative features and it is in its total relationship to the rest of the handwriting that its significance lies, particularly in regard to the signature.

Both male and female symbols within the copybook *I* rest upon the writing "reality" baseline. The strength of the male (father) figure symbolically correlates with here-and-now practicality emphasized by mid-zone placement. The leftward stroke indicates a metaphorical going-back toward the past and beginnings which involve a family figure. Activity prevails as the stroke turns sharply rightward toward the future, into the area of integration. The male symbol carries within it both hard and soft strokes, symbolic of male procreation and active thrust.

The concept of the dynamic father-provider, trainer of the young and role-model to both sexes is expressed essentially by the forward motion to the right, as well as placement in the middle zone. Psychologically, ideal guidance by the male provides both affection and discipline as the child moves into the future. In primitive societies both past and present, the care of infants and small children lies with the mother and other female tribal members, but the father and other male members assume responsibility for training sons when they reach a certain age. The father-male role embodies action.

Clarification of the background of male-female symbolism requires exploring the anthropological, philosophical and psychological history of what it means to be male or female. In forming the personal pronoun *I*, it appears logical that certain strokes embody emotional and physical responses. It seems reasonable to believe that the writing of so personal a gesture as the letter which uniquely stands for the self offers particular clues to the total self-image. *The ppI is different from the capital I.*

Both generally and specifically, handwriting patterns reflect social, psychological and cultural changes affecting the writer. Counterparts of earlier responses exist in all we do, even during change. How we feel about ourselves is reflected in every aspect of our biological being, and how we choose to exist in our social and sexual relationships is crucial to feelings of self-worth.

In these matters, the why of the *I* has much to tell us.

A GLOSSARY OF *I*'S

The following categories offer a simplified overview of various ego symbols. They are not to be construed as a final or last word in the analysis of the self, but merely as clues in assessing the writer's personality . . . guideposts which may point in certain directions.

The acquisitive I: crowded, hooked, inflated lower loop.

The adaptable I: curved, lightly pressured, moderate in size.

The aggressive I: angular, forward slanted, speedy, heavily pressured, rising on baseline.

The aesthetic I: harmoniously proportioned, original, artistic in form, well spaced, simplified, very fine or pastose line.

297

The cautious I: arcade, circled or retraced.

 The conforming I: Either copybook or taught print-script, evenly pressured, moderate speed, evenly spaced, moderate size and slant, legible, rounded.

The contrary I: reversed-written.

 The courageous I: Tall, heavily pressured, large in size, angular.

The demanding I: space-taking.

 The depressed I: small, pressed down, descending baseline, isolated, lightly pressured.

The emotional I: acutely reclined, heavily pressured, below or above baseline, flourished.

The energetic I: ascending, large, rapid, horizontal pressure.

The enthusiastic I: ascending, underlined, heavily pressured, large in size and scope, flourished, connected to other words, right-tending.

The fearful I: small size, uneven pressure, tremor, fragmented, leftward movement, irregular placement, changing size, slowness, arcade.

The independent I: non-conforming shapes, tall, leftward motion, printed *I*, reversed *I*.

The modest I: copybook or simple forms, moderate or small size, consistency.

The number-minded I: ego symbol in the design of money or numerals.

The reserved I: Vertical or leftward slant, medium or small size, retraced or squeezed formation, left-tending.

The showmanship I: largeness in height and scope, involved ornaments, wide spacing.

A SENTENCE COMPLETION FORM

A form with thirty-one sentences to be completed in writing was the beginning of the author's investigations of the pp*I*. Subsequent studies have verified the first indication of the special significance of the written *I*.

The following group of handwritings belongs to adolescent boys in a junior high school who were placed in an Experience Center. The Center was geared to help behavior problems within the classroom with special tutoring and attempts at therapy.

Each handwriting shows disturbance in the self-image. Most of these boys had poor relationships with their parents. Many of them are dyslexic—unable to read properly—although their intelligence has been rated average or above. Each handwriting generally shows severe disturbance.

As a communication device in the counseling situation, handwriting analysis offers fruitful ground for further investigation. Each boy in this particular study was eager to have the analyst discuss his handwriting.

It is possible that earlier attempts at evaluating the self-image of each boy might have helped avert mistaken goals and self-defeating behavior. To the trained graphologist, these handwritings cry, "Help!"

301

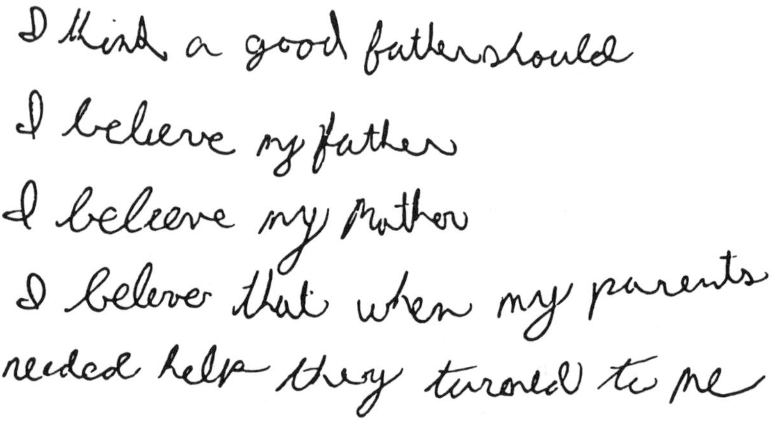

I think a good father should

I believe my father

I beleeve my mother

I belever that when my parents
needed help they turned to me

Fig. 208

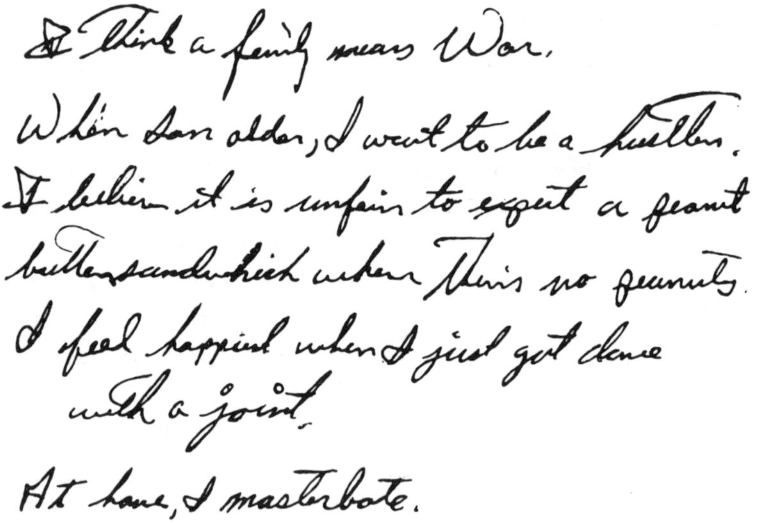

I think a family means War.

When I am older, I want to be a husller.

I believe it is unfair to expect a peanut
butter sandwich when theirs no peanuts.

I feel happiest when I just got done
with a joint.

At home, I masterbate.

Fig. 209

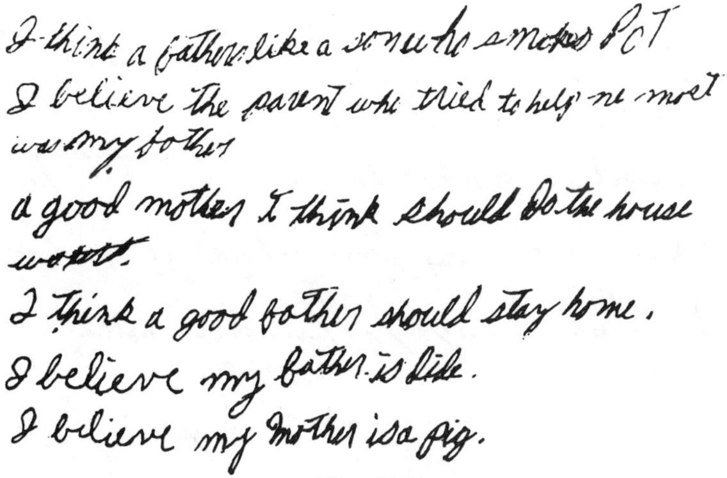

I think a father like a son who smokes POT
I believe the parent who tried to help me most
was my father

a good mother I think should do the house
work.
I think a good father should stay home.
I believe my father is dead.
I believe my mother is a pig.

Fig. 210

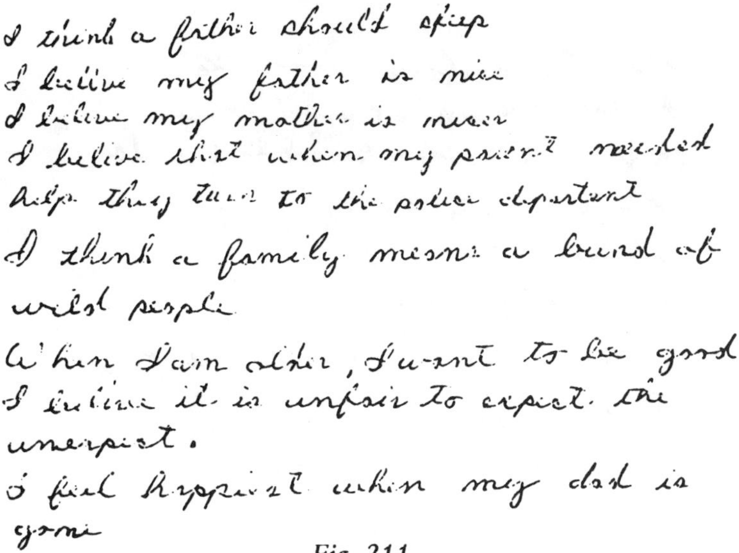

I think a father should sleep
I believe my father is nice
I believe my mother is nicer
I believe that when my parent needed
help they turn to the police department
I think a family means a bunch of
wild people
When I am older, I want to be good
I believe it is unfair to expect the
unexpect.
I feel happiest when my dad is
gone

Fig. 211

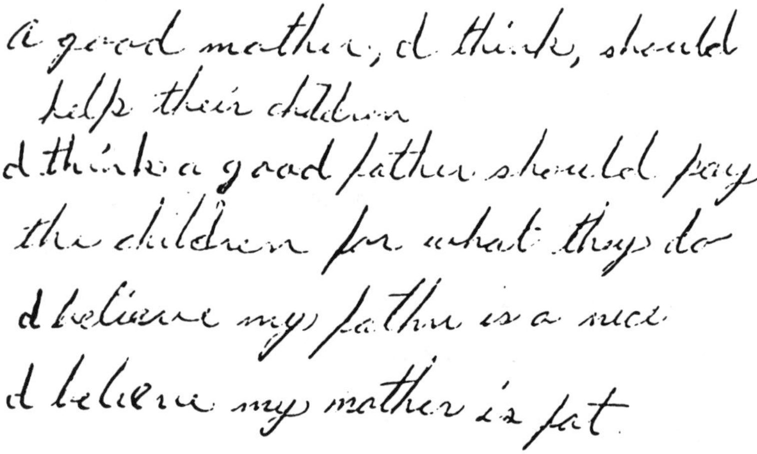

a good mother, I think, should
help their children
I think a good father should pay
the children for what they do
I believe my father is a nice
I believe my mother is fat

Fig. 212

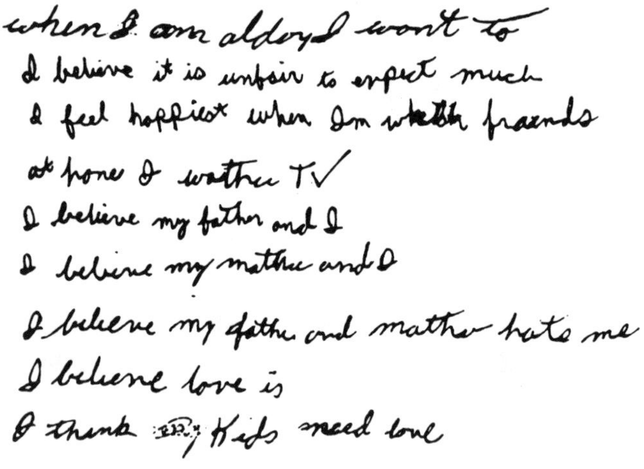

when I am older I won't to
I believe it is unfair to expect much
I feel happiest when I'm with friends
at home I watch TV
I believe my father and I
I believe my mother and I
I believe my father and mother hate me
I believe love is
I think my kids need love

Fig. 213

BIBLIOGRAPHY

Adler, Alfred. *Theory and Practice of Individual Psychology.* Humanities Press, New York, 1951.

Allport, Gordon. *Pattern and Growth in Personality.* Holt, Rinehart & Winston, New York, 1961.

    Studies in Expressive Movement. Macmillan Company, New York, 1933.

Ansbacher, H. L. and R. *The Individual Psychology of Alfred Adler.* Harper & Row, New York, 1967.

Anthony, Daniel. *The Graphological Psychogram, Psychological Meaning of Its Sectors and Symbolic Interpretation of Its Indicators.* 92 Mt. Vernon Place, Newark, New Jersey 07106.

Arnheim, Rudolf. *Art and Visual Perception.* University of California Press, Berkeley, 1971.

Cattell, Raymond B. *Personality and Motivation Structure and Measurement.* World Book Co., Yonkers-on-Hudson, 1957.

Dreikurs, Rudolph. *Children: The Challenge.* Meredith Press, New York, 1964.

    Equality: The Challenge of Our Times. Meredith Press, New York, 1961.

Erikson, Erik. *The Challenge of Youth.* Anchor-Double-day, New York, 1965.

———. *Childhood and Society.* Norton C. Norton, New York, 1964.

Hartford, Huntington. *You Are What You Write.* Macmillan Publishing Co., Inc., New York, 1973.

Hearns, Rudolph. *Handwriting, An Analysis Through Its Symbolism.* Vantage Press, New York, 1966.

Horney, Karen. *Neurosis and Human Growth.* W. W. Norton & Co., New York, 1950.

Kellogg, Rhoda, & O'Dell, Scott. *The Psychology of Children's Art.* CRM, Random House, New York, 1967.

Konopka, Gisela. *The Adolescent Girl in Conflict.* Prentice-Hall, New York, 1966.

Marcuse, Irene. *Guide to the Disturbed Personality through Handwriting.* Arco Publishing Co., New York, 1969.

Maslow, Abraham. *Toward a Psychology of Being.* Von Nostrand Reinhold Co., New York, 1968.

Mendel, A. O. *Personality in Handwriting.* Stephen Daye Press, New York, 1947.

Olyonova, Nadya. *Handwriting Tells.* Bobbs-Merrill Company, New York, 1969.

Piaget, Jean. *The Origins of Intelligence in Children.* International University Press, New York, 1966.

Roman, Clara. *Handwriting, A Key To Personality.* Noonday Press, Farrar, Strauss & Giroux, New York, 1962.

———. *Encyclopedia of the Written Word.* Frederick Ungar Publishing Co., Inc., New York, 1968.

Satir, Virginia. *Conjoint Family Therapy*. Science & Behavior Books, Inc., Palo Alto, Calif., 1967.

Saudek, Robert. *The Psychology of Handwriting*. George Allen & Unwin, Ltd., London, 1954.

Schofield, William. *Psychotherapy: The Purchase of Friendship*. Spectrum Books, Prentice-Hall, New York, 1964.

Sonnemann, Ulrich. *Handwriting Analysis as a Psychodiagnostic Tool*. Grune & Stratton, New York, 1964.

Teltscher, Dr. Herry O. *Handwriting–Revelation of Self*. Hawthorn Books, Inc., N. Y., 1971.

Towle, Charlotte. *Common Human Needs*. National Association of Social Workers, Inc., New York, 1965.

Whitehead, Alfred North. *Symbolism, Its Meaning & Effect*. Macmillan Company, New York, 1927.

Wolff, Werner. *Diagrams of the Unconscious*. Grune & Stratton, New York, 1948.
Journal of Aesthetics and Art Criticism
Journal of Perceptual and Motor Skills
Journal of Projective Techniques

Additional References used for Second Edition:

Campbell, Joseph: *The Masks of God,* Viking Press, Inc., New York, 1959.

Clynes, Manfred: Sentics: *The Touch of Emotions,* Anchor Press/Doubleday, New York, 1977.

Rubin, Roger; "Identifying the Mother and Father in Handwriting," Monograph, National Society for Graphology, New York.

Stone, Merlin: *When God Was a Woman,* Dial Press, New York, 1976.

PAGE INDEX TO FIGURE ILLUSTRATIONS IN PARTS I-III

Index courtesy of Ann Wintrode

JANE NUGENT GREEN holds a Master's Degree in Social Work (MSW) from the University of Minnesota. She graduated Phi Beta Kappa from the University of Iowa. Her C.G. was obtained from the Minnesota Association of Handwriting Analysis. Former long-time faculty member of the Alfred Adler Institute of Minnesota, and active in the Alliance for the Mentally Ill, she has presented Workshops and taught communication dynamics as well as analytic graphology. Published works in psychology journals include articles on counseling, communication skills, and the self-image. She is a member of the American Association of Handwritings Analysts.

Important differences between the written personal pronoun I and the capital I are now evident. Your readable book offers new concepts . . . real assets to graphologists on both sides of the Atlantic.
Jane Paterson, Author, Handwriting Consultant, England

Accurate handwriting analysis has potential to

identify strengths and weaknesses
uncover trouble spots
offer incentive to change undesirable habits
increase awareness of hidden creativity

YOU AND YOUR PRIVATE I is divided into four main sections:

The Written Self-Image is an understandably written introduction to the basic principles of handwriting analysis offering an overview of the development of the self-image.

Male-Female Symbolism Within the I presents newly discovered graphic elements concerning male-female factors within the *I* as they relate to the writer's self-concept, sexual identity and relationships.

The Evolving Self applies principles of the first two sections to actual case histories illustrating human development from child to adult.

Changing the Self-Image contains detailed case studies which demonstrate how analytic graphology helps in obtaining a useful diagnosis of personality. This section also demonstrates specific processes of improving the self-image through changing parts of your handwriting.